A Guide for Substitute and Interim Teachers

If you are a substitute or interim teacher, or thinking of becoming one, you won't want to miss the techniques and strategies in this user-friendly, easy-to-read handbook. Author Barbara Washington guides you through every step, including the application process, lesson planning, classroom management, and school safety. Each chapter offers practical examples and current best practices to support you on your way to success. The book also includes essential tools such as reproducible lesson plans, worksheets, graphic organizers, and more. Concise but complete, this is an ideal resource for substitute teacher professional development.

Barbara Washington is an educator with more than three decades of teaching experience. She holds an M.Ed. and has earned teacher certifications in three states. She has written teacher training modules, procedures manuals, and curricula for various high school technology courses. The author now works primarily in adult education and remains fully committed to the science of education.

A Guide for Substitute and Interim Teachers

Practical Tools for Success

Barbara Washington

Routledge
Taylor & Francis Group

NEW YORK AND LONDON

First published 2021
by Routledge
52 Vanderbilt Avenue, New York, NY 10017

and by Routledge
2 Park Square, Milton Park, Abingdon, Oxon, OX14 4RN

Routledge is an imprint of the Taylor & Francis Group, an informa business

Library of Congress Cataloging-in-Publication Data
Names: Washington, Barbara, author.
Title: A guide for substitute and interim teachers : practical tools for success / Barbara Washington.
Identifiers: LCCN 2020033997 | ISBN 9780367559465 (hardback) | ISBN 9780367559243 (paperback) | ISBN 9781003095798 (ebook)
Subjects: LCSH: Substitute teaching—Handbooks, manuales, etc. | Substitute teachers—In-service training.
Classification: LCC LB2844.1.S8 W37 2021 | DDC 371.14/122—dc23
LC record available at https://lccn.loc.gov/2020033997

ISBN: 978-0-367-55946-5 (hbk)
ISBN: 978-0-367-55924-3 (pbk)
ISBN: 978-1-003-09579-8 (ebk)

Typeset in Palatino
by Apex CoVantage, LLC

Visit the eResources: www.routledge.com/9780367559243

Dedication

Dedicated to the one and only Marshall Thomas Washington whose patient support made this work possible.

Contents

eResources

The lesson plans, handouts, and figures in this book are also available as free eResources on our website, so you can easily print them for classroom use. Please go to the book's product page, www.routledge.com/9780367559243, and click on the link for Support Material. You'll then find the full set of eResources.

The Author

Barbara Washington is an educator with more than three decades of teaching experience. She holds an M.Ed. and has earned teacher certifications in three states. Barbara loves teaching, has taught secondary teacher education, and also taught for more than two decades at the high school level. She also enjoys writing teacher education materials and has written teacher training modules, procedures manuals, and curricula for high school technology courses. Barbara has facilitated new teacher training, professional development seminars, and has been a sought-after substitute teacher for grades K–12 in recent years. Her passion for education, love of teacher training, and exceptional ability to engage learners continue to be the author's motivation to contribute to the literature on teaching and learning. The author now works primarily in adult education and remains fully committed to the science of education.

Figures and Tables

Figures

Tables

Preface

Welcome to what I hope will be a delightful read on the way to enjoy a successful experience and make a positive impact on the students in your care during your days as a substitute or interim teacher. First, please understand that you are an indispensable member of the school's faculty and no school can run smoothly without your presence. As long as there are brick-and-mortar schools, there will be a need for substitute teachers. Your job is to be the students' teacher during the absence of the regular teacher, which is an awesome responsibility. Although your stay may be temporary, it is no less important than the permanent teachers and staff. In this book, I use the terms "interim" and "substitute" interchangeably. *Interim*, as you know, means temporary or in the meantime. For me, *interim teacher* sometimes expresses more accurately the level of responsibility, expertise, and professionalism needed to perform the duties of the job effectively.

Next, thank you for putting yourself out there to take on the challenges of substitute teaching. It takes special people with a commitment and caring for others to do this job well. I have done the job too, so I know the ups and downs, the good and the challenging. So, if no one else takes the time to thank you during your tenure as an interim teacher, I thank you today. Just as the school's principals and teachers perform highly critical functions, so do the substitute teachers. Your time, talent, and expertise help the school to run more efficiently, and no school can operate effectively without you.

Substitute teachers are in very high demand. Recently, I heard of a district that had to begin a school year with more than 50 long-term substitute teachers, so the value of good interim teachers cannot be overestimated. As you establish good working relationships, you will probably find that teachers request you by name to substitute for them. The goal of this book is to give you the tools you'll need to be a highly qualified substitute teacher who will be able to fill this critical need.

Finally, you will find everything you need to be a successful interim teacher within the pages of this guide. This handbook provides valuable insight into the art of teaching, the process of learning, and the value of education. It is designed to assist all interim teachers at every grade level from K–12 in public schools, charter schools, and private schools. The principles covered also apply to any subject, class, or course content. You will succeed with a great deal of focus, keen observation skill, and above-average communication skill.

You have already demonstrated your determination to be successful by taking the time to read through this guide. The students and teachers need you; the staff and administrators need you; and the world of education needs you. Whether you are a recent graduate preparing to begin a teaching career, a retired educator, or working as a substitute for some other reason, may your journey into interim teaching be a joyous, productive, and successful time in your life, and happy teaching!

Acknowledgments

Thank God for the inspiration and determination to complete this project.

A great big thank you to substitute and interim teachers across the nation who show up every day and assist students to make progress academically and developmentally. Yours is too often a thankless job, and you are all true heroes in my book.

Finally, thanks to the publishers of this brief but important work. Your confidence in the need for and importance of this project will go a long way in helping substitute and interim teachers to do their work more competently, professionally, and successfully.

1

Working in Schools

Train up a child in the way he should go and when he is old, he will not depart from it.

King Solomon[1]

The Benefits of Substitute Teaching

Congratulations on your decision to work as a substitute teacher, and welcome to the profession! Teaching is often very rewarding. One of its greatest benefits is the opportunities you will have to help young people learn and make a positive impact on their lives. Another great advantage is the ability to set your own work schedule. There are many rewards and benefits of substitute teaching, including the following, to name just a few:

- ◆ Setting your own work schedule
- ◆ Selecting your preferred school(s)
- ◆ Choosing the grade, subject, and class you prefer
- ◆ Being in high demand
- ◆ Earning a high salary (in some locations)
- ◆ Earning health benefits (in some locations)
- ◆ Getting prepared for a permanent teaching position
- ◆ Enjoying a variety of activities
- ◆ Staying active as a retired educator
- ◆ Helping students to learn

Teaching can be both exhilarating and exhausting as well as rewarding and challenging. But I think the benefits far outweigh the challenges. Although the duties include teaching, protecting, and supervising children all day, you will enjoy the energy and enthusiasm that young people bring. While your day may involve a lot of standing or walking, you will be perfectly fine. At times, a first grader may need you to wipe his/her nose, sixth-grade students may exhibit boundless energy, and an eleventh-grade student may challenge your authority, but sometimes a challenge can be good for the soul. You might have to make your way through a large building to get to your next class within four minutes or less. No worries—you will make it there on time, and you will be that much closer to getting in 10,000 steps when you arrive! You might have to carry the equipment in Phys Ed class or help feed the rabbits in Animal Science class in the barn. Even so, you will still have the advantage of being able to choose which class suits you the best. Simply consider your own strengths, personality, and age/stage, and you will thoroughly enjoy the journey ahead. Table 1.1 summarizes some of the characteristics of those who make the best, most sought-after, and most successful substitute teachers.

Table 1.1 Characteristics of Successful Substitute Teachers

Patient	Excellent communicators	Dependable
Reliable	Resilient	Punctual
Ability to teach	Enjoy young people	Adaptable
Flexible	Excellent people skills	Confident
Sense of humor	Good listeners	Attentive
Technology literate	Compassionate	Problem-solving skills
Attention to detail	Goal oriented	Professional attitude

The Application Process

Once you have decided in which school or school district you want to work, you are ready to start the application process. Most schools and districts require that you have a high school diploma, and most use an online application process. Some large school districts employ a third-party education placement service to screen, hire, and place their substitute teachers, and most placement services utilize an online application process as well. The online application usually requires proof of education and certifications. There are school districts that also require substitutes to have a substitute teaching certificate or substitute permit as well. To be eligible for a substitute teaching certificate or permit, applicants are usually required to have at least 60 college credits.

In addition, schools are required to conduct thorough background and health screening for all new hires, including the substitute staff. It will generally take three or more weeks to obtain the documentation and clearances to complete the application process, and there are fees involved as well. Many schools, districts, and placement services also require applicants to attend one or more orientation sessions before they are officially hired. Table 1.2 outlines the paperwork and other items that are typically needed to complete the entire process to become a substitute teacher.

Table 1.2 Employment Application Documents

Application form	FBI fingerprint clearance
Application letter	Sexual misconduct clearance
Resume	Medical form and TB test result
Reference letters	Employment eligibility verification
High school diploma/transcript	W-4
College transcript(s)	Other forms such as:
Professional certificate(s)	Workers' compensation form
Criminal background check	Code of ethics form
Child abuse clearance	Employee acknowledgment form

Accepting Assignments

Once you are officially signed on as a substitute teacher, you will be able to accept work assignments. Assignments vary in length from one day up to those lasting weeks or even months, as shown in Table 1.3. Substitute teachers are needed to fill in when the regular teacher is absent, and the reasons for teacher absences vary, with some of the most common reasons included in the following list:

◆ Sick leave
◆ Personal leave
◆ Family leave
◆ Bereavement
◆ Professional development
◆ Peer visits
◆ Field trips
◆ Meeting attendance
◆ Position vacancies

Some schools allow their substitutes to remain on the active list if they work at least once a month, whereas some education placement agencies require their substitutes to work at least three days a week to remain on the active list. Since substitute teachers fulfill the role of teachers, they should try to accept assignments that match their skill sets, areas of interest, and expertise. For recent graduates who are starting their teaching careers, interim and substitute teaching is an excellent way to learn about potential job vacancies. In addition, many retired teachers enjoy substituting for the flexibility of choosing their own work schedule while earning extra income during their retirement years.

The pay rate for per diem assignments averages around $100/day. Long-term assignments average about $200/day because long-term substitute teachers usually develop lesson plans, teach content, and perform testing and grading as well. School districts generally pay more for those holding teaching certification, and the larger school districts tend to have higher pay scales. In some places, substitutes can earn close to $300/day.

In addition, many schools and districts utilize online absence management systems, in which the regular teacher enters the date(s) of the anticipated absence electronically. The substitute teacher is given access to the system, logs in, and accepts assignments from those that are posted. This is a convenient way to schedule assignments, and online absence management is becoming the prevailing method for scheduling substitute staff because the system can be accessed 24 hours a day, seven days a week.

Finally, sometimes substitutes may find it rewarding to limit themselves to working for one school or school district exclusively because this maximizes their ability to understand the school's students, staff, and room locations. The more familiar the staff and students are with you (and you with them), the more they will be able to trust you as a reliable and competent substitute for the regular teacher. I have seen substitutes who worked mainly for one school or district subsequently hired in permanent positions in their schools.

Table 1.3 Lengths of Interim Teaching Assignments

Per diem	Assignment lasts for one school day or less
Multiday	Assignment lasts for two to five school days
Long-term	Assignment lasts for five or more consecutive school days

The School Environment

Public schools are frequently organized into geographic districts that are governed by state boards of education. They work with a local school board and have a superintendent and other administrative staff performing the top leadership responsibilities. The building principal heads the individual school, and s/he may have several assistant principals who supervise the various departments. Figure 1.1 depicts a typical organizational structure for public school districts. Large urban, public school districts may operate hundreds of schools, so they provide more work opportunities for substitute teachers. In large schools, there could 100 or more teaching staff, so interim teachers may find themselves substituting in many different courses and subject areas.

Charter schools are run by private boards and have different accountability requirements than public schools do. Charter schools were developed to increase the options and alternatives for public school education, and the president or head of school is in charge of the school. Private schools offer their own unique approaches to education, are not funded by tax dollars, and may not be subject to the same regulations that govern public and charter schools. Note Figures 1.2 and 1.3 for examples of the typical organizational structures for private and charter schools.

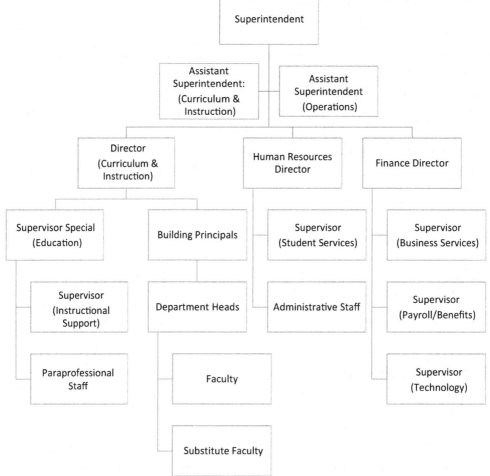

Figure 1.1 Typical Organizational Chart—Public School District

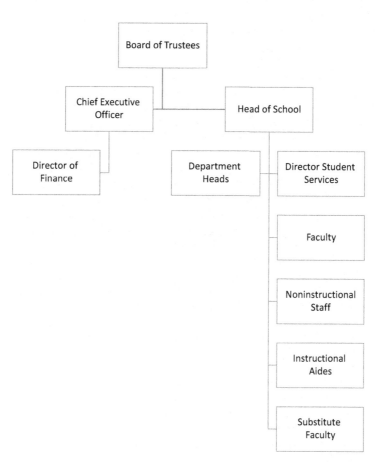

Figure 1.2 Typical Organizational Chart—Charter School

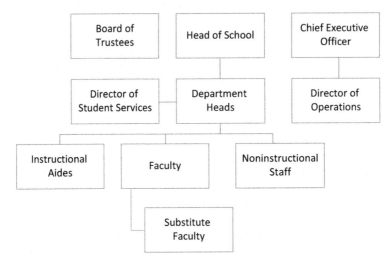

Figure 1.3 Typical Organizational Chart—Private School

Schools are organized into various departments, with a faculty member leading as the department head or lead teacher. In addition, teachers may work in teams by grade level or subject. Sometimes, different grades are located in separate hallways, floors, or parts of the building (referred to as *pods*). Teachers of the same grades or subjects form professional learning communities (PLCs) for the purpose of collaboration and improvement of teaching practice.

Most states mandate that students must attend school for at least 180 days a year. Keep a copy of the school's calendar for the year to stay informed of the days when school is closed. Also, determine how the school notifies its substitutes of unexpected school closures due to inclement weather. The school year usually starts in August or September, ends in May or June, and includes several holidays/breaks during the year as shown in Table 1.4.

In addition to the regular bell schedule, there are a variety of other schedules, including delayed opening, early dismissal, half day, etc. If possible, obtain copies of the school's various bell schedules, and be careful to start and dismiss your classes according to the schedule for the day. Also, large schools may have more than one lunch period, and you should go to lunch according to your teacher's schedule. Sometimes, schools also alternate what classes students attend on certain days of the week, such as A day or B day schedules, and someone should notify you upon arrival if that is the case. Note the examples of typical school hours illustrated in Table 1.5 and the regular bell schedule for a public high school in Table 1.6.

Table 1.4 Typical School Holidays

Description	Month	Length in Days
Professional development	Varies	5–10
Labor Day	September	1
Jewish holidays	October	2
Columbus Day	October	1
Veterans Day	November	1
Winter break	December	7–14
Martin Luther King Day	January	1
Presidents' Day	February	1
Spring break	March/April	7–10
Memorial Day	May	1

Table 1.5 Typical School Hours

Elementary school	8:45 a.m.–3:45 p.m.
Middle school	7:30 a.m.–2:30 p.m.
High school	7:30 a.m.–2:30 p.m.

Table 1.6 Typical Bell Schedule in Middle and High Schools

Period	Start Time	End Time	Length
1	7:30 a.m.	9:05 a.m.	95 min.
2	9:10 a.m.	10:45 a.m.	95 min.
3	10:50 a.m.	12:55 p.m.	125 min.
A Lunch	10:50 a.m.	11:20 a.m.	30 min.
Class (A)	11:25 a.m.	12:55 p.m.	90 min.
B Lunch	11:30 a.m.	12:00 p.m.	30 min.
Class (B)	10:50 a.m.	12:55 p.m.	125 min.
C Lunch	12:25 p.m.	12:55 p.m.	30 min.
Class (C)	10:50 a.m.	12:55 p.m.	125 min.
4	1:00 p.m.	2:30 p.m.	90 min.

In schools, it seems that no two days are the same. Every day is different, bringing its own unique set of joys and challenges. Learn to expect the unexpected. At times, schools are noisy—especially during arrival, dismissal, and movement between classes. At other times, there will be announcements via the public address system or calls on the classroom phone. Sometimes, classes move outdoors for fire drills, gym classes, or science experiments. There will be assemblies in the auditorium, pep rallies in the gym, and trips to the library or computer lab. Remain flexible and prepared for a variety of incidental occurrences that are all a part of a normal day in school.

Grade Levels

Substitute teachers should enjoy working with young people and have a basic understanding of human growth and development. Many develop a

Table 1.7 Typical Student Age by Grade Level

Level	Grade(s)	Age Range
Prekindergarten	Pre-K	3–5 years
Elementary/primary	K–5	5–10 years
Middle school	6–8	11–13 years
High school	9–12	14–17 years

preference for working in either elementary (primary) school, middle school, or high school and tend to be more effective working with their preferred grade level as noted in Table 1.7.

Subjects/Courses

As you know, students are required to study the major (or core) subjects: English, Mathematics, Science, and Social Studies. They are also required to study Health and Physical Education and some form of the arts such as Music or Art. High school courses can be semester-long, half-year, or full-year courses, and schools offer a wide range of course electives in addition to the major subjects. In addition, high school courses are assigned a specific number of credits each. Some courses earn one credit, while other courses earn half a credit. Advanced placement (AP) courses may offer more than one credit each and college credit as well. Students must accumulate a minimum number of credits in high school to qualify for graduation, and that total varies among both states and public, charter, and private schools. According to the U.S. Department of Education's National Center for Education Statistics (Digest of Education Statistics, 2013), U.S. public high schools required 19 total credits on average for graduation. Charter school graduation requirements are comparable to public schools, and private schools tend to require slightly more credits for graduation than both charter and public schools. Table 1.8 contains a list of the typical course offerings from elementary through high school. Table 1.9 lists the typical high school course electives (U.S. Department of Education, Studies of High School Transcripts, 2009).

Table 1.8 Typical Subjects/Courses

Elementary School	Middle School	High School
Reading	English / Language Arts	English / Language Arts
Writing	Introduction to Algebra	Algebra 1 / Algebra 2
Math	Introduction to Geometry	Geometry
Science	U.S. History	Trigonometry/Calculus
Social Studies	Geography	U.S. History
Health / Phys Ed	Science	World History
Computer Literacy	Earth and/or Physical Science	U.S. Government
The Arts	Health / Phys Ed	Biology
	The Arts	Chemistry
	Foreign Languages	Physics
	Computer Literacy	Earth Science
	Other electives	Foreign Languages
		Health / Phys Ed
		Fine and Performing Arts
		Other electives

Table 1.9 High School Course Electives

Agricultural Science	Family and Consumer Science
Architecture	Foreign Languages
Business and Management	Allied Health
Business and Office	Industrial Arts
Marketing and Distribution	Law
Communications	Military Science
Computer Science and Technology	Visual and Performing Arts
Education	Vocational Education

Source: U.S. Department of Education, National Center for Education Statistics, Studies of High School Transcripts, 2009

Working With Students

In a school, adults are in a child's world. Students are developing, growing, and gradually maturing into adults, and, of course, the adults must be patient with the process. In general, the older the student, the more mature s/he will be, but children mature at different rates. It is helpful to be familiar with the stages of human development and to have a general understanding of where students may be developmentally. You will find recommendations on some great resources on human development in the Recommended Resources at the end of this guide.

Successful substitute teachers also understand a basic principle of education: **all children can learn**. You may be called on to serve students with special needs and challenges to learning or those who are gifted learners. Embrace the fact that all children can learn, and you will find success. Remain flexible, adaptable, and comfortable working with anyone without regard to ability or disability, race or nationality, gender or beliefs, etc. See subsequent chapters for specific details to improve your ability to work well with all of your students.

Working With School Staff and Community

Interim teachers are required to have the ability to work cooperatively with all members of the school staff and community. It is important to understand that you play a vital role and you are an integral part of the success of the school team. Develop an excellent working relationship with the staff, and keep all of your interactions positive and professional. Treat each person with the same courtesy and respect with which you expect and deserve to be treated. Arrive on time (or a few minutes early) and stay until the end of the day. Follow dress codes and all policies and procedures. Avoid using school equipment for personal reasons, and, of course, always keep personal issues or problems out of the workplace. Stay helpful and flexible, and try not to refuse reasonable requests from the staff.

Teachers sometimes work in teams within the same classroom, so there may be times when substitutes will work with other teachers and/or paraprofessionals in the classroom. At those times, it is important to know when to take the lead (and when to allow the team teacher to lead). Determine this by checking with the team teacher or paraprofessional (para). Most times, the para or team teacher will take the lead and ask you to assist as needed. At other times, you may be asked to lead the class. Be prepared for both leading and serving as the assistant.

On rare occasions, you may have contact with parents or relatives of the students. Interim teachers in long-term assignments may be required to conduct parent conferences to discuss student grades and/or behavior. Keep these encounters positive with the understanding that all members of the school community are on the students' side. Never allow any interaction to become adversarial or combative. Even if you must discuss missed work, failed tests, or misbehavior, assure parents and relatives that student progress is assured as long as the school team, the student, and his/her family continue to work together.

Also, teachers frequently have extra duties in addition to teaching their classes. These extra duty assignments assist the school administrators to run schools more efficiently. Substitute teachers are expected to also attend their teacher's extra duty assignments, which may include hall duty, lunch/cafeteria duty, bus duty, or some other extra duty assignment.

Hall Duty

To monitor school hallways, teachers may be assigned to take a station in a certain hallway location. Usually, a chair or desk is positioned where the teacher can monitor hallway activity and check the hall passes of any students in the halls when classes are in session.

Lunch/Cafeteria Duty

Sometimes, teachers are needed to monitor students at lunch in the cafeteria. Elementary or middle school teachers may have to escort their students to and from lunch. Lunch duty may require assisting with students lining up, getting their lunches, and/or discarding trash.

Bus Duty

If the teacher has bus duty, s/he may need to escort students to their buses or see that students exiting the school building board their buses safely. Stay in position until all students have boarded safely, and wait for a staff member to confirm that your bus duty is completed.

Other Extra Duty Assignments

Other types of extra duty assignments can include assisting in the main office, the guidance office, the library, the school store, or some other location in the school.

Ten Basic Rules for Working in Schools

Of course, follow the same basic protocols in school that you would follow in any workplace. Substitute teachers are members of the professional staff and their professionalism should always be apparent. There are specific guidelines, however, that are unique to working in school settings. Here are ten important rules for staff conduct in schools:

Rule #1. Do not leave your class unattended.
Rule #2. All children can learn.

Rule #3. Know the school's emergency procedures.

Rule #4. Always protect every student's privacy and confidentiality.

Rule #5. Take attendance. Account for all students.

Rule #6. Respect students' right to use the restroom or see the nurse.

Rule #7. Do not ignore serious bullying or aggressive behavior.

Rule #8. Do not disrespect, ridicule, or threaten students.

Rule #9. Do not touch students.

Rule #10. Do not interact with students on social media.

First Day Checklist

The following checklist will get you off to a good start on your first day and every day.

- ◆ Arrive on time, and park in spaces designated for substitute teachers.
- ◆ Follow the established sign-in procedure.
- ◆ Proceed to your assigned classroom promptly.
- ◆ Locate and review all of the following:
  - ● Emergency folder, lesson plan, teacher's schedule, attendance sheets
- ◆ Note the location of handouts, textbooks, and student supplies such as pens, paper, etc.
- ◆ Follow the established bell schedule—start and end class on time.
- ◆ Record attendance neatly and accurately.
- ◆ Follow the assigned lesson plan.
- ◆ Keep students working and maintain order throughout the class session.
- ◆ Closely monitor student movement in and out of the classroom.
- ◆ Return promptly from lunch or other breaks.
- ◆ Attend the teacher's extra duty assignments (if any).
- ◆ Put the classroom in order.
- ◆ Follow established dismissal procedures.
- ◆ Leave feedback for the teacher.
- ◆ Secure the classroom and follow the established exit procedure.

Note

1 Scripture taken from the Holy Bible, New King James Version®. Copyright © 1982 by Thomas Nelson. Used by permission. All rights reserved.

References

Digest of Education Statistics. U.S. Department of Education. National Center for Education Statistics (NCES). 2013. Retrieved June 21, 2020, from nces.ed.gov./programs/digest.

Holy Bible, King James Version. Proverbs 22:6. King Solomon. 1000 BC.

Studies of High School Transcripts. 2009. U.S. Department of Education, National Center for Education Statistics (NCES). Retrieved May 11, 2020, from nces.ed.gov.

2

Planning and Preparation

- The Importance of Planning
- Planning Lessons
- Backup Plans
- Set Yourself Up for Success
- Reproducible Lesson Plans and Worksheets
- Reproducible Graphic Organizers

The Importance of Planning

Planning lessons is a significant part of a teacher's responsibility, and the ability to plan lessons effectively is included in teacher performance evaluations. Good lesson planning takes time, skill, and effort. Effective lessons plans are like points on a map that move students along a continuum of learning in a given subject area, so the lesson plan guides student learning, progress, and achievement. Successful substitute/interim teachers make every effort to follow the lesson plan explicitly so that students continue to make progress during the regular teacher's absence. Good substitutes also do their best to make sure that students have something productive to do even if a lesson plan is not available.

Planning Lessons

The format used for lesson plans varies among schools, but the lesson plan should include the lesson goal, essential question, learning activities, and related resources needed. Directions should be clear, and supplemental resources should be provided if referenced in the plan. Most schools also require teachers to provide a set of emergency lesson plans for unplanned absences in addition to those for planned absences. The emergency plans are usually kept in a designated place such as a substitute folder or an emergency folder.

Make it a practice to follow the lesson plan carefully. Read over the plan at least twice. Review it after the students begin working. Make additional announcements as needed to cover anything that was overlooked. It is important to explain all of the lesson directions to the class and to clarify instructions as needed to make sure everyone understands. The students will appreciate your desire to do a good job, so do not hesitate to make corrections or clarifications if necessary.

Backup Plans

Occasionally, a backup lesson plan may be needed. If you cannot locate the lesson plans, consult the department head, a teacher of the same subject, or an instructional aide. You might need to be prepared with your own ideas and activities for students to do if the lesson plan is not available. If students are busy with classwork, they are easier to supervise, so prepare a folder that you

Table 2.1 Class Activities for Backup Lesson Plans

Crossword puzzles	Subject-specific worksheets	Story time
Spelling bee	Geography bee	History bee
Cryptograms	Board games	Silent reading
Fold-and-pass writing game	Maps to label/color	Card games
Graphic organizers	Drawing/coloring activities	Letter writing

Table 2.2 Websites Offering Free Downloads for Teachers

Kids.gov	Loc.gov/teachers (Library of Congress)
Edsitement.neh.gov	Nasa.gov/stem/foreducators/k-12
Artsedge.kennedy-center.org/educators/lessons	Nga/education/learningresources
Commonlit.org	Nationalgeographic.org/education
Commonsense.org	Nytimes.com/section/learning
Educationworld.com	Mpt.pbslearningmedia.org
Teach-nology.com	Weareteachers.com

can bring with you containing copies of worksheets, crossword puzzles, word searches, etc. Table 2.1 contains some great ideas for backup lesson activities, and there are many websites that offer free downloads of lessons, worksheets, and other activities, some of which are noted in Table 2.2. In addition, reproducible, ready-to-use lesson plans, worksheets, and graphic organizers are also provided for your convenience at the conclusion of this chapter.

Long-term substitute teachers are frequently required to develop the lesson plans themselves. Sometimes, the regular teacher will work in close coordination with his/her substitute to develop and implement the lesson plans. If not, the substitute should seek assistance with planning lessons from a department head or another teacher of the same subject. Consult the curriculum map if one is available since the curriculum map is an outline of the learning plan for a course by month, semester, or school year.

Lesson plans are submitted to a supervisor or department head at least one week before the planned lesson. There is normally a designated planning period during the school day for teachers to plan and prepare their lessons. Use this time to prepare and review your plans, make copies, and assemble any materials needed to make the lesson a success. In addition to the planning period, some schools also have a common planning period so teachers can collaborate with each other about upcoming lessons.

Finally, there may be times when students have completed the assigned work for the day, with more than ten minutes of class time remaining. In many schools, teachers are required to do bell-to-bell instruction and use every available minute of class time for some type of teaching or learning activity. For this reason, students may have a warmup or do-now activity to complete at the beginning of a class and/or an exit ticket or sponge activity at the end of a class. Warmups and do-nows are lesson starters, while exit tickets are lesson summaries. Sponge activities are short activities designed to soak up a few leftover minutes at the end of a lesson before the dismissal bell.

For your convenience, there are several reproducible and ready-to-use lesson plans, worksheets, and graphic organizers provided at the end of this chapter. Included are lesson plans for Mathematics, English / Language Arts, Science, and Social Studies for elementary, middle, and high school, as summarized in Table 2.3. Feel free to make copies as needed to help your students stay productive and engaged in learning.

Set Yourself Up for Success

There is often a lack of accountability for substitute and interim teachers, which has caused many substitutes to feel it is not their job to plan lessons or to actually teach. But notice that the position title is substitute or interim *teacher*—with the operative word being *teacher*, not substitute *babysitter* or substitute *friend*. The position you are accepting is that of a teaching substitute—a qualified and capable stand-in for the person who teaches.

Unfortunately, there are substitute teachers who think it is fine to preside over "free days" in which the students do nothing productive toward the lesson goals. Some have promoted this false image of substitute teachers through their lack of concerted efforts to assist or teach. These substitutes will give the assignment and then basically ignore the students for the rest of the class and remain at the teacher's desk reading a novel or catching up on their email, etc. They will allow students to do nothing for an entire 90-minute class whether a lesson plan is available or not. That loss of 90 minutes times 30 students equals 2,700 minutes, which is 45 whole hours of lost learning!

I am a realist, so I do understand that on rare occasions, free days do happen in schools, but the students should not learn to expect one *every time* they have a substitute teacher. It *is* the substitute teacher's job to work hard at helping students to complete the learning activities. It is the substitute's job to do his/her very best and to teach if and when the lesson calls for it. Also, it is the substitute's responsibility to prepare backup lesson plan activities just in case and to also know some basics about teaching and learning. I appeal to every substitute teacher to rise to the occasion and dispel the myth that when students see you, they automatically think "free day." In life, free is rarely really free—there is usually a cost hidden somewhere. Do not just preside over students losing time—if necessary, plan lessons and teach.

I encourage you also to set yourself up for success before your scheduled assignments by getting a few things prepared to bring along with you. Being ready will boost your confidence and increase your chances of successfully managing any challenges that the day may bring. Note the following list of recommended items to bring with you just in case:

- Backup lesson plans
- Activities or worksheets (30 copies of each)
- Two or three sponge activities
- Dry-erase board markers
- Dry-erase board eraser
- Clipboard
- Lined paper
- Sharpened pencils
- Pens
- Portable pencil sharpener
- Paper clips
- Notebook
- Timekeeping device
- Sticky notes
- Portable hand sanitizer
- Portable disinfectant wipes
- Personal bottled water
- Lunch/snack

REPRODUCIBLE LESSON PLANS AND WORKSHEETS

Table 2.3 List of Reproducible Lesson Plans and Worksheets

Grade Level	Subject	Lesson Title	Accompanying Worksheet(s)
2–3	Math	Reproducible Lesson Plan #1: Count to 100 by 5s and 10s	Figure 2.1
3–5	ELA	Reproducible Lesson Plan #2: Frequently Confused Words	Figure 2.2 Figure 2.3
2–5	Science	Reproducible Lesson Plan #3: What's the Weather Forecast Today?	
2–5	Social Studies	Reproducible Lesson Plan #4: Respect for Others' Rights, Opinions, Property	
6–8	Math	Reproducible Lesson Plan #5: Dividing Multidigit Numbers	Figure 2.4 Figure 2.5
6–8	ELA	Reproducible Lesson Plan #6: Breakfast Is the Most Important Meal of the Day	Figure 2.6
6–8	Science	Reproducible Lesson Plan #7: Earth's Place in the Universe	
6–8	Social Studies	Reproducible Lesson Plan #8: A Look at the Constitution	Figure 2.7
9–12	Math	Reproducible Lesson Plan #9: Interpreting Quantitative Data	Figure 2.8 Figure 2.9
9–12	ELA	Reproducible Lesson Plan #10: Writing With Variety and Interest	
9–12	Science	Reproducible Lesson Plan #11: Digital Transmission and Storage of Information	Table 2.4
9–12	Social Studies	Reproducible Lesson Plan #12: A Comparison of Cultural Distinctions	

REPRODUCIBLE LESSON PLAN #1

ELEMENTARY SCHOOL GRADES 2–3*   MATHEMATICS LESSON PLAN

Lesson: Count to 100 by 5s and 10s.

Essential Question: How do you count to 100 by 5s and 10s?

Objective: Students will be able to count to 100 by 5s and 10s.

Duration: Approximately 60 minutes

Resources:

Board (white or chalk)

Board markers or chalk

Number line display poster

Small manipulatives (chips, blocks, buttons, etc.)

Teacher-made worksheet (Figure 2.1)

Pencils

Agenda:

1. Introduce the lesson by counting aloud by 5s as you point to each number on the number line display.
2. Explain the idea of counting by 5s.
3. Ask for volunteers to come to the board and count by 5s. Point to the numbers on the display as each student counts.
4. Distribute manipulatives and ask the students to place them in groups of five.
5. Repeat the process to introduce and practice counting by 10s.
6. Clean up and put away the manipulatives.
7. Have the students complete the Count to 100 by 5s and 10s worksheet.

Assessment:

Completed worksheets (Figure 2.1)

*Note: This lesson can be adjusted for grades K–1 by decreasing the complexity (i.e., count to 25). The lesson can be adjusted for grades 4–5 by increasing the complexity (i.e., count to 200).

REPRODUCIBLE WORKSHEET FIGURE 2.1

COUNT TO 100 BY 5s AND 10s WORKSHEET

PLACE THE CORRECT NUMBER IN EACH BLANK SPACE WHEN **COUNTING BY 5S.**

1) 5 ____ 15 ____ 25 ____ 35 ____ 45 ____ 55 ____ 65 ____ 75 ____ 85 ____ 95 ____

2) 10 ____ 20 ____ 30 ____ 40 ____ 50 ____ 60 ____ 70 ____ 80 ____ 90 ____ 100

3) 15 ____ 25 ____ 35 ____ 45 ____ 55 ____ 65 ____ 75 ____ 85 ____ 95 ____

4) 20 ____ 30 ____ 40 ____ 50 ____ 60 ____ 70 ____ 80 ____ 90 ____ 100

5) 25 ____ 35 ____ 45 ____ 55 ____ 65 ____ 75 ____ 85 ____ 95 ____

PLACE THE CORRECT NUMBER IN EACH BLANK SPACE WHEN **COUNTING BY 10S.**

6) 10 ____ 30 ____ 50 ____ 70 ____ 90 ____

7) 20 ____ 40 ____ 60 ____ 80 ____ 100

8) 30 ____ 50 ____ 70 ____ 90 ____

9) 40 ____ 60 ____ 80 ____ 100

10) 50 ____ 70 ____ 90 ____

Figure 2.1 Count to 100 by 5s and 10s Worksheet

REPRODUCIBLE LESSON PLAN #2

ELEMENTARY SCHOOL GRADES 3–5   ENGLISH / LANGUAGE ARTS LESSON PLAN

Lesson: Use frequently confused words correctly in sentences.

Essential Question: How do I determine which frequently confused word is correct to use in a sentence?

Objectives:

1. Students will learn the meanings of frequently confused words.
2. Students will select the correct frequently confused word in each of several sentences.

Duration: 60 minutes

Resources:

Board (white or chalk)

Board markers or chalk

Teacher-made worksheet (Figure 2.2)

Paper

Pencils

Agenda:

1. Write three sentences on the board as follows:
   "Each child had _____ (to, too, two) colored pencils."
   "I will get some cereal when I go _____ (to, too, two) the store."
   "There was _____ (to, too, two) much noise in the cafeteria."
2. Explain the differences between *to*, *too*, and *two* and the importance of choosing the correct spelling of frequently confused words. Emphasize that the correct choice depends on the meaning of the words and the context of the sentence.
3. Ask the students to choose the correct word for each sentence on the board.
4. Use Q&A and discussion to convey the meanings of the frequently confused words on the teacher-made worksheet (Figure 2.2).
5. Give the students a two-minute brain break while you distribute the worksheets (Figure 2.2).
6. Have the students complete one or two sentences and review the correct answers with the class.
7. Have the students work in pairs or individually to complete the worksheet. Circulate around, assisting and encouraging.

Assessment: Completed worksheets (Figure 2.3)

REPRODUCIBLE WORKSHEET FIGURE 2.2

FREQUENTLY CONFUSED WORDS WORKSHEET

Underline the correct word in parentheses, and then write your choice in the blank space.

1. The suitcase was (two, to, too) heavy for her to carry. _____
2. Jason, isn't it (you're, your) turn to take out the trash? _____
3. Antonio had (no, know) pencils in his pencil case. _____
4. Malissa likes to (by, buy) her electronics online. _____
5. The show will last for about one (hour, our). _____
6. They moved to the country because of the (peace, piece) and quiet. _____
7. Sit where you will be able to (hear, here) the teacher clearly. _____
8. (It's, Its) best to read your work carefully before you hand it in. _____
9. (Meat, Meet) us by the fountain in the center of the mall. _____
10. When (there, they're their) is silence, we can begin. _____
11. Jeremy takes his dog for a walk every day of the (week, weak). _____
12. The winning team wore (there, they're, their) uniforms today. _____
13. We will take a snack break at (two, to, too) o'clock. _____
14. Nathan (threw, through) the ball as far as he could. _____
15. Let's get ready to go (two, to, too) recess now. _____
16. Raise your hand quietly if you (no, know) the answer. _____
17. Today, let's all sit (hear, here) by the window for story time. _____
18. After the parade passed (by, buy), we all got ice-cream cones. _____
19. Everyone in the class received a (peace, piece) of candy. _____
20. As you walk (threw, through) the hallway, please do not talk. _____

Figure 2.2 Frequently Confused Words Worksheet

REPRODUCIBLE WORKSHEET FIGURE 2.3

FREQUENTLY CONFUSED WORDS WORKSHEET ANSWER KEY

Underline the correct word in parentheses, and then write your choice in the blank space.

1.	The suitcase was (two, to, <u>too</u>) heavy for her to carry.	**too**
2.	Jason, isn't it (you're, <u>your</u>) turn to take out the trash?	**your**
3.	Antonio had (<u>no</u>, know) pencils in his pencil case.	**no**
4.	Malissa likes to (by, <u>buy</u>) her electronics online.	**buy**
5.	The show will last for about one (<u>hour</u>, our).	**hour**
6.	They moved to the country because of the (<u>peace</u>, piece) and quiet.	**peace**
7.	Sit where you will be able to (<u>hear</u>, here) the teacher clearly.	**hear**
8.	(<u>It's</u>, Its) best to read your work carefully before you hand it in.	**It's**
9.	(Meat, <u>Meet</u>) us by the fountain in the center of the mall.	**Meet**
10.	When (<u>there</u>, they're their) is silence, we can begin.	**there**
11.	Jeremy takes his dog for a walk every day of the (<u>week</u>, weak).	**week**
12.	The winning team wore (there, they're, <u>their</u>) uniforms today.	**their**
13.	We will take a snack break at (<u>two</u>, to, too) o'clock.	**two**
14.	Nathan (<u>threw</u>, through) the ball as far as he could.	**threw**
15.	Let's get ready to go (two, <u>to</u>, too) recess now.	**to**
16.	Raise your hand if you (no, <u>know</u>) the answer.	**know**
17.	Today, let's all sit (hear, <u>here</u>) by the window for story time.	**here**
18.	After the parade passed (<u>by</u>, buy), we all got ice-cream cones.	**by**
19.	Everyone in the class received a (peace, <u>piece</u>) of candy.	**piece**
20.	As you walk (threw, <u>through</u>) the hallway, please do not talk.	**through**

Figure 2.3 Frequently Confused Words Worksheet Answer Key

REPRODUCIBLE LESSON PLAN #3

ELEMENTARY SCHOOL GRADES 2–5   SCIENCE LESSON PLAN

Lesson: What's the Weather Forecast Today?

Essential Question: What are the climate differences in different parts of the world?

Objective: Students will compare and contrast the differences in climate based on location.

Resources:

Photos of four locations: two in warm climates and two in cold climates

Old magazines

Flip chart paper, poster board, or construction paper

Paper

Scissors

Pencils, crayons, colored pencils

Duration: 60 minutes

Agenda:

1. Show photos of the different parts of the world and ask students to guess their locations.
2. Discuss the meaning of *climate* and climate differences based on location.
3. Hold a Q&A discussion on climate in different parts of the world.
4. Divide the students into pairs.
5. Distribute flip chart paper, poster board, or construction paper to each pair of students. Tell the students to draw a middle line to separate the paper into two halves.
6. Direct the students to write words, draw or cut out pictures, and/or color two different locations: one warm climate and one cold climate.
7. Allow sufficient cleanup time.

Assessment:

Q&A period about locations and their climates using student posters

REPRODUCIBLE LESSON PLAN #4

ELEMENTARY SCHOOL GRADES 2–5   SOCIAL STUDIES LESSON PLAN

Lesson: Civics Lesson on Respect for Others' Rights, Opinions, Property

Essential Question: What are the foundations of a civil society in the U.S.?

Objective: Students will demonstrate respect for their classmates' rights in a group activity.

Duration: Approximately 60–90 minutes

Resources:

Board (white or chalk)

Board markers or chalk

Construction paper

Scissors

Letter stencils

Pencils, crayons, colored pencils, markers

Agenda:

1. Write the words *respect*, *rights*, *opinions*, and *property* on the board.
2. Lead a discussion about respect, rights, opinions, and property.
3. Distribute supplies.
4. Divide students into groups of four.
5. Each group member takes a word: respect, rights, opinions, property.
6. Each student stencils, colors, and decorates his/her word.
7. Provide a brain or snack break.
8. Circulate around, assist, and encourage, making a note of high levels of cooperation and respect.
9. Commend high levels of respect for the rights, opinions, and property that you observed in the classroom during this lesson.
10. Allow sufficient cleanup time.

Assessment:

1. Create a classroom display.
2. Have a few volunteers present their work to the class.

REPRODUCIBLE LESSON PLAN #5

MIDDLE SCHOOL GRADES 6–8   MATHEMATICS LESSON PLAN

Lesson: Dividing Multidigit Numbers

Essential Question: How do you divide multidigit numbers using the standard algorithm?

Objective: Students will divide multidigit numbers using the standard algorithm.

Duration: 60 minutes

Resources:

Board (white, chalk)

Board markers or chalk

Teacher-made worksheet (Figure 2.4)

Pencils, paper

Agenda:

1. Review the standard algorithm for dividing multidigit numbers: Divide, Multiply, Subtract, Bring Down (DMSB)
2. Write two demonstration problems on the board and have student volunteers work through them one at a time as you explain the DMSB process.

   Demo Problem 1   Demo Problem 2
   5)905   12)48,144

   Demo 1 Answer = 181   Demo 2 Answer = 4,012

3. Distribute the teacher-made worksheet (Figure 2.4).
4. Tell the students to complete the first two or three problems.
5. Review the first two or three completed problems with the class.
6. Have the students complete five or six problems.
7. Give the students a brain break of one to two minutes.
8. Review one more problem solution at the board.
9. Have the students complete the remaining worksheet problems.
10. Circulate to assist, correct, and encourage.

Assessment: Completed worksheets (Figure 2.5)

REPRODUCIBLE WORKSHEET FIGURE 2.4

DIVIDING MULTIDIGIT NUMBERS WORKSHEET

Solve the problems below without a calculator by using the Divide, Multiply, Subtract, Bring Down method.

ANSWERS

1. 2)1,806   _____

2. 3)3,699   _____

3. 5)1,505   _____

4. 7)4,214   _____

5. 4)6,488   _____

6. 9)7,227   _____

7. 8)24,040   _____

8. 10)15,500   _____

9. 12)36,480   _____

10. 11)441,188   _____

Figure 2.4 Dividing Multidigit Numbers Worksheet

REPRODUCIBLE WORKSHEET FIGURE 2.5

DIVIDING MULTIDIGIT NUMBERS WORKSHEET ANSWER KEY

Solve the problems below without a calculator by using the Divide, Multiply, Subtract, Bring Down method.

	ANSWERS
1. 2)$\overline{1,806}$	**903**
2. 3)$\overline{3,699}$	**1,233**
3. 5)$\overline{1,505}$	**301**
4. 7)$\overline{4,214}$	**602**
5. 4)$\overline{6,488}$	**1,622**
6. 9)$\overline{7,227}$	**803**
7. 8)$\overline{24,040}$	**3,005**
8. 10)$\overline{15,500}$	**1,550**
9. 12)$\overline{36,480}$	**3,040**
10. 11)$\overline{441,188}$	**40,108**

Figure 2.5 Dividing Multidigit Numbers Worksheet Answer Key

REPRODUCIBLE LESSON PLAN #6

MIDDLE SCHOOL GRADES 6–8   ENGLISH / LANGUAGE ARTS LESSON PLAN

Lesson: Breakfast Is the Most Important Meal of the Day

Essential Question: How do I support an argument with reasons and evidence?

Objective: Students will write a three-paragraph persuasive essay to support their opinion on the importance of breakfast in relationship to other meals.

Resources:

Computers with word processing software (if available)

Pens/pencils and lined paper (if no computers are available)

Persuasion map graphic organizer (Figure 2.6)

Duration: 90–120 minutes

Agenda:

1. Lead a Q&A: Do you think breakfast is the most important meal of the day? Why or why not?
2. Discuss the meaning of *argument*, *reasons*, and *relevant evidence*.
3. Distribute persuasion map graphic organizers (Figure 2.6).
4. Review the writing process:
   – Prewriting/Planning
   – Drafting
   – Revising/Editing
   – Presenting
5. Explain the assignment: Write or type a three-paragraph persuasive essay to support your opinion about the importance of breakfast. Organize your essays as follows:
   Paragraph 1: Intro and opinion (3+ sentences)
   Paragraph 2: Reasons for the opinion with evidence (4+ sentences)
   Paragraph 3: Summary and conclusion (4+ sentences)
6. Circulate around to assist and encourage as students complete the steps in the writing process to prepare their essays.

Assessment:

Completed essays with good organization, clear writing, logical reasoning, and strong evidence

Student_____Persuasive Essay Title_____

Introduction and Claim

Reason #1	Reason #2

Supporting Evidence	Supporting Evidence

Supporting Evidence	Supporting Evidence

Conclusion

Figure 2.6 Persuasion Map Graphic Organizer

REPRODUCIBLE LESSON PLAN #7

MIDDLE SCHOOL GRADES 6–8

SCIENCE LESSON PLAN

Lesson: Earth's Place in the Universe

Essential Question: What is Earth's place in the universe?

Objective: Create a graphical illustration of the planets in the solar system.

Resources:

Computer access to the Internet and presentation software

Poster or other illustration of the planets

Poster board, flip chart paper, or construction paper

Pencils, colored pencils, crayons, markers

Duration: 90–120 minutes

Agenda:

1. Display and discuss the Earth's place in the solar system.
2. Students research individually for illustrations of the Earth in the solar system.
3. Give students the option of working with a partner or individually to:
   a) Create a short slide presentation (4–5 slides) illustrating the solar system.

   or

   b) Draw and color an illustration of the solar system.
4. Allow sufficient cleanup time.

Assessment:

Students present their illustrations to the class

REPRODUCIBLE LESSON PLAN #8

MIDDLE SCHOOL GRADES 6–8   SOCIAL STUDIES LESSON PLAN

Lesson: A Look at the Constitution

Essential Question: What is the purpose of the Constitution of the U.S.?

Objective: Students will determine the purpose of the Constitution by learning the Preamble.

Duration: 60 minutes

Resources:

Large poster displaying the Preamble to the Constitution

Copies (class quantity) of the preamble (Figure 2.7)

Pencils, pens, lined paper

Agenda:

1. Lead a Q&A to introduce the Constitution.
2. Distribute copies of the Preamble (Figure 2.7).
3. Read the Preamble aloud.
   "We the People of the United States, in Order to form a more perfect Union, establish Justice, insure domestic Tranquility, provide for the common defense, promote the general Welfare, and secure the Blessings of Liberty to ourselves and our Posterity, do ordain and establish this Constitution for the United States of America." (uscourts.gov)
4. Discuss a few (or all) of the main themes in the Preamble:

We the People	United States	More perfect Union
Establish Justice	Insure Tranquility	Common defense
General Welfare	Liberty	Posterity

5. Have students copy the Preamble neatly onto lined paper.
6. Have students work with a partner to memorize the Preamble as you circulate, assist, and encourage.

Assessment:

Write the Preamble from memory

REPRODUCIBLE WORKSHEET FIGURE 2.7

"We the People of the United States, in Order to form a more perfect Union, establish Justice, insure domestic Tranquility, provide for the common defense, promote the general Welfare, and secure the Blessings of Liberty to ourselves and our Posterity, do ordain and establish this Constitution for the United States of America."

. . . .

"We the People of the United States, in Order to form a more perfect Union, establish Justice, insure domestic Tranquility, provide for the common defense, promote the general Welfare, and secure the Blessings of Liberty to ourselves and our Posterity, do ordain and establish this Constitution for the United States of America."

. . . .

"We the People of the United States, in Order to form a more perfect Union, establish Justice, insure domestic Tranquility, provide for the common defense, promote the general Welfare, and secure the Blessings of Liberty to ourselves and our Posterity, do ordain and establish this Constitution for the United States of America."

. . . .

"We the People of the United States, in Order to form a more perfect Union, establish Justice, insure domestic Tranquility, provide for the common defense, promote the general Welfare, and secure the Blessings of Liberty to ourselves and our Posterity, do ordain and establish this Constitution for the United States of America."

. . . .

"We the People of the United States, in Order to form a more perfect Union, establish Justice, insure domestic Tranquility, provide for the common defense, promote the general Welfare, and secure the Blessings of Liberty to ourselves and our Posterity, do ordain and establish this Constitution for the United States of America."

Figure 2.7 Preamble to the Constitution Reproducible Master
Source: uscourts.gov

REPRODUCIBLE LESSON PLAN #9

HIGH SCHOOL GRADES 9–12   MATHEMATICS LESSON PLAN

Lesson: Interpreting Quantitative Data

Essential Question: How do I accurately interpret quantitative data in spreadsheet graphs or charts?

Objective: Students will input, manipulate, and interpret quantitative data using the formula, function, and graph features of spreadsheet software.

Duration: 90–120 minutes

Resources:

Computers with access to spreadsheet software

Teacher-made worksheet (Figure 2.8)

Agenda:

1. Give a practical example of the importance of the ability to accurately interpret quantitative data (ideas for examples include surveys, opinion polls, class averages, etc.).
2. Have students start the spreadsheet software as you distribute worksheets (Figure 2.8).
3. Explain worksheet directions.
4. Encourage to collaborate with a partner.
5. Circulate around and assist/encourage as the students input data, create formulas and charts, interpret the data, and answer the analysis questions.

Assessment:

Completed spreadsheets with embedded charts and correct answers to analysis questions (Figure 2.9).

REPRODUCIBLE WORKSHEET FIGURE 2.8

INTERPRETING QUANTITATIVE DATA WORKSHEET

1. Create an electronic spreadsheet for an imaginary class of ten students.
2. Enter student names and test grades.
3. Use the formulas or function feature to create the test averages column.
4. Use the insert chart function to create a column chart of the class averages.
5. Answer the analysis questions.

FIRST NAME	LAST NAME	TEST1	TEST2	TEST3	TEST4	AVERAGES
Sample	Student1	68	76	77	82	
Sample	Student2	90	87	78	88	
Sample	Student3	73	59	67	70	
Sample	Student4	92	91	89	94	
Sample	Student5	74	76	79	70	
Sample	Student6	83	82	88	84	
Sample	Student7	80	66	62	81	
Sample	Student8	78	79	77	85	
Sample	Student9	55	60	57	62	
Sample	Student10	59	61	56	52	

PLACE THE COLUMN CHART HERE (SEE STEP 4)

Analysis Questions

1. What is the median test average?
2. What is the lowest average?
3. What is the highest average?
4. What does the chart indicate
   about the class averages?

Figure 2.8 Interpreting Quantitative Data Worksheet

INTERPRETING QUANTITATIVE DATA WORKSHEET ANSWER KEY

1. Create an electronic spreadsheet for a class of 10 students.
2. Enter student names and test grades.
3. Use the formulas or function feature to create the test averages column.
4. Use the insert chart function to create a column chart of the class averages.
5. Answer the analysis questions.

FIRST NAME	LAST NAME	TEST1	TEST2	TEST3	TEST4	AVERAGES
Sample	Student1	68	76	77	82	76
Sample	Student2	90	87	78	88	86
Sample	Student3	73	59	67	70	67
Sample	Student4	92	91	89	94	92
Sample	Student5	74	76	79	70	75
Sample	Student6	83	82	88	84	84
Sample	Student7	80	66	62	81	72
Sample	Student8	78	79	77	85	80
Sample	Student9	55	60	57	62	59
Sample	Student10	59	61	56	52	57

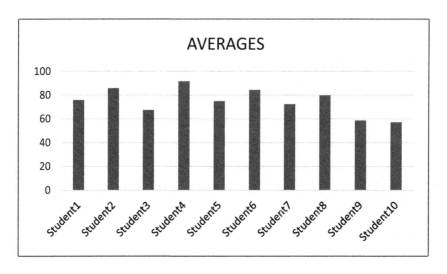

Analysis Questions

1. What is the median test average?	75
2. What is the lowest average?	57
3. What is the highest average?	92
4. What does the chart indicate about the class averages?	The class average shows that the class is understanding at the C grade level

Figure 2.9 Interpreting Quantitative Data Worksheet Answer Key

REPRODUCIBLE LESSON PLAN #10

HIGH SCHOOL GRADES 9–12   ENGLISH / LANGUAGE ARTS LESSON PLAN

Lesson: Writing With Variety and Interest

Essential Question: How do I use a variety of phrases and clauses to add interest to my writing?

Objective: Students will write advertising copy that has variety and captures audience interest.

Duration: 90 minutes

Resources:

Wording for popular commercial advertisements

Computer with word processing software

Pens, lined paper

Agenda:

1. Lead a discussion on the wording of popular commercial advertisements.
2. Discuss a few ways to add variety and interest to writing and speaking, such as adjectives, adverbs, pauses, inflection, images, etc.
3. Ask students to decide on a product or service they would like to write about.
4. Directions: Write the copy for a one-minute advertisement for a student-selected product or service using variety to capture audience interest and attention.
5. Circulate around and assist/encourage as students practice their ads in groups of three to four.
6. Have a few students present their ads to the class.

Assessment:

Summary question: Name two ways in which you added variety and interest to your ad.

REPRODUCIBLE LESSON PLAN #11

HIGH SCHOOL GRADES 9–12   SCIENCE LESSON PLAN

Lesson: Digital Transmission and Storage of Information

Essential Question: Do the advantages of digital transmission and storage of information outweigh the disadvantages?

Objective: Students will create a slide presentation examining the advantages and disadvantages of the digital transmission and storage of information.

Duration: 90–120 minutes

Resources:

Computer with access to the Internet and presentation software

Grading rubric (Table 2.4)

Agenda:

1. Lead a Q&A discussion about the conflict between Earth's natural resources versus the human need for technology.
2. Ask students if they believe the advantages of using natural resources to advance technology outweigh the disadvantages.
3. Distribute and discuss grading rubric (Table 2.4).
4. Students work in groups of two or three to create multi-slide presentations to present their opinion as follows:
   a. Title slide
   b. Natural resources (definition and advantages: 2 slides)
   c. Digital transmission / data storage (definition and advantages: 2+ slides)
   d. Natural resources versus digital transmission / data storage (disadvantages: 2+ slides)
   e. Student opinion (1–2 slides)
   f. Conclusion (1 slide)
5. Submit slide notes. Present group findings to class if time permits.

Assessment:

Grading rubric (Table 2.4)

Table 2.4 Grading Rubric for Slide Presentations

	Excellent	Good	Fair	Needs Improvement
Slide design and legibility	Attractive with excellent balance of text and graphics	Good appearance, balance, legibility	Fair legibility, appearance	Design, layout, or other elements detract from slide legibility
Natural resources slides	Comprehensive descriptions including several clear advantages # of slides = 3+	Good descriptions with at least two advantages # of slides = 2+	Description lacks clarity; less than two advantages # of slides = 2	Weak/ description; no advantages mentioned # of slides = 1
Digital transmission slides	Comprehensive descriptions including several clear advantages # of slides = 3+	Good descriptions with at least two advantages # of slides = 2+	Description lacks clarity; less than two advantages # of slides = 2	Weak/ description; no advantages mentioned # of slides = 1
Opinion slide	Logical argument with very strong support # of slides = 2+	Logical argument with good support # of slides = 2	Argument supported # of slides = 1	Argument not logical; no support # of slides = 1
Grammar/ mechanics	No errors in mechanics	Less than four errors in mechanics	Less than six errors in mechanics	Several distracting errors in mechanics

REPRODUCIBLE LESSON PLAN #12

HIGH SCHOOL GRADES 9–12   SOCIAL STUDIES LESSON PLAN

Lesson: A Comparison of Cultural Distinctions

Essential Question: How does culture influence social interaction?

Objective: Students will develop a comparison guide that highlights the differences between two cultures.

Duration: 90 minutes

Resources:

Photos of examples of different cultures

Computers with Internet access

Flip chart paper or poster board

Pencils, colored pencils, markers

Agenda:

1. Lead a Q&A discussion on the meaning of *culture*, *cultural differences*, and reasons for those differences.
2. Students form groups of two to four.
3. Explain that they should create a two-column display comparing and contrasting two different cultures. Students should research styles of dress, food, occupation, recreation, etc.
4. Students' posters should highlight the differences between the cultures.
5. Display posters in classroom.
6. Allow sufficient time for cleanup.

Assessment: Students discuss their findings with the class.

Reproducible Graphic Organizers

Table 2.5 List of Reproducible Graphic Organizers

Figure 2.10	KWL Chart
Figure 2.6	Persuasion Map
Figure 2.11	Venn Diagram

TOPIC_____

K What I Know	W What I Want to Know	L What I Learned

Figure 2.10 KWL Chart Graphic Organizer

Student_____Persuasive Essay Title_____

Introduction and Claim

Reason #1		Reason #2

Supporting Evidence		Supporting Evidence

Supporting Evidence		Supporting Evidence

Conclusion

Figure 2.6 Persuasion Map Graphic Organizer

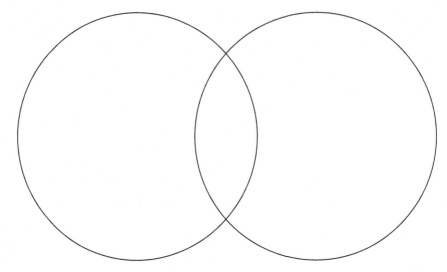

Figure 2.11 Venn Diagram Graphic Organizer

Reference

The U.S. Constitution: Preamble. United States Courts. Retrieved May 29, 2020, from uscourts.gov/about-federal-courts/educational-resources/.

3

Teaching, Learning, and Assessment

- Teaching Strategies
- Learning Principles
- Technology in Education
- Diverse Learners
- Grading
- Testing
- Standardized Assessment

Teaching Strategies

This brief overview of effective teaching techniques will give you a competitive edge as a *highly qualified* substitute or interim *teacher*. The chapter covers a general overview of teaching, learning, and assessment and starts with a brief discussion of pedagogy—the method and practice of teaching.

Teaching is both a perfected art and a learned skill. In some ways, teaching can be thought of as a calling to service, duty, and responsibility. Good teachers share knowledge, ideas, concepts, principles, data, and information in a way that makes it as easy as possible for learners to understand, apply, and use that knowledge later. Teachers are responsible for facilitating learning for every one of their students every day, and effective teaching requires preparation and practice. Teachers must navigate through the needs of many to reach each student right where s/he is, which is why effective teachers use a wide variety of teaching strategies.

There are many ways that teachers deliver instruction, and classroom instruction has evolved from teacher-centered delivery methods to more student-centered, active-learning instructional models. Long lectures have been replaced by shorter and more interactive explanations of lesson concepts and ideas. Teachers have become the facilitators of learning. They provide the student-centered activities and then coach the students through the learning activities toward the desired learning goals. Teachers encourage students to think critically and analytically, and many also implement metacognition strategies that teach students to consider how they think and process information. Educational technology, peer teaching/coaching, and cooperative learning have made students active participants who often share in the decisions with teachers about how the lessons will be taught and learned.

TeachThought, a premier provider of innovation in K–12 education, published a list of instructional strategies that summarize current best practices in teaching (32 Research-Based Instructional Strategies, 2020). These strategies exemplify the principles of effective instructional delivery, and a few of them are included in Table 3.1 as a reference for some of the most effective teaching methods in current use.

Table 3.1 Research-Based Instructional Strategies

Setting Clear Goals and Objectives	Effective Feedback
Reinforcing effort and providing recognition	Low-threat assessment
Cooperative learning	Higher-level questioning
Direct instruction	Directed reading-thinking activity
Individualized instruction	Anticipation guides
Identifying similarities and differences	KWL charts
Summarizing and note-taking	Scaffolding instruction

Source: TeachThought Staff, TeachThought.com, February 2, 2020

Learning Principles

Learning is the acquisition of knowledge or skills through instruction, study, or experience. It is good when students can recall facts and understand ideas and concepts, but learning targets are aimed at getting students to retain what has been learned at a deeper level. The ultimate goal is that students will internalize content and have the ability to use what they have learned to analyze problems, develop unprecedented solutions, and innovate new ideas. The real measure of successful learning is that students are either career or college ready and committed to lifelong learning at the end of their K–12 education.

Presently, teachers are implementing a wide variety of creative and individualized strategies to maximize learning for their students. This is important since students have unique abilities, learning strengths, learning weaknesses, and learning styles. Effective learning activities involve the use of as many of our five senses as possible, and students retain more for longer periods of time when they are presented with the information in a variety of ways. Active learning is the basic principle underlying the use of multiple types of learning activities that result in student engagement, increased retention, and higher-order thinking. For example, the use of graphic organizers is widespread because they help students to organize their thoughts, plan out processes, and visualize relationships. Graphic organizers are useful across subjects and disciplines to improve reading comprehension, writing ability, and reasoning ability. Table 3.2 outlines a few of the popular graphic organizers that are having a positive impact on the learning process. Also, feel free to reproduce and use Figures 2.6, 2.10, and 2.11 as needed (located at the end of Chapter 2).

Cooperative learning (Kagan and Kagan, 2013) is a popular learning strategy that is also widely used to get students actively involved in the lesson

Table 3.2 Popular Graphic Organizers

KWL chart	Prereading graphic that utilizes students' prior knowledge
Anticipation guide	Prereading graphic used to arouse interest in the reading
Story map	Graphic for identifying the elements of a story (plot, characters, etc.)
Sequence chart	Graphic for identifying the steps in a process, timelines, elements in a sequence
Persuasion map	Graphic for organizing the claim and supporting evidence when writing a persuasive essay
DRTA (directed reading thinking activity)	Strategy to increase reading comprehension by having students make predictions about a passage and confirm or deny their predictions after reading
Vocabulary organizer	Graphic used to increase understanding of vocabulary words
Venn diagram	Graphic used to compare/contrast similarities and differences

Table 3.3 Kagan Cooperative Learning Strategies

Timed-Pair-Share	RoundRobin	Numbered Heads Together
Find Someone Who	Find-the-Fiction	Stand-up-Hand-up-Pair-up
Corners	Inside-Outside Circle	Quiz-Quiz-Trade
RallyCoach	Mix-Pair-Share	Fan-N-Pick

Source: Kagan Cooperative Learning, Kagan and Kagan, 2013

activities. With cooperative learning, students are encouraged to collaborate with each other, and the classroom seating arrangements are designed to encourage this collaboration. Cooperative learning strategies promote student focus, discussion, interaction, and interest in the lesson. Some of Kagan's most popular strategies are illustrated in Table 3.3.

Technology in Education

The use of traditional textbook, pen, and paper has diminished in favor of the use of technology for every part of the learning process and at every grade level from K to 12. Technology in education continues to expand, and substitute teachers can expect to see students using everything from digital textbooks to virtual learning to countless types of interactive software. Entire textbooks are now available online, and, in most places, each student has access to a desktop or laptop computer. Technology in education has opened up limitless possibilities for students, and they can now access information on any subject from any location at any time. It has literally made the universe available to students, and the expectation is that the use of technology for learning will continue to increase.

Teachers use technology to deliver instruction in a wide variety of ways. Teaching hardware includes interactive smartboards and projection devices that enable teachers to display their computer screens for instruction. Testing has gone online as well. In many states, elementary and middle students now take state standardized tests on computers, and many high school courses include online testing as well. There is educational software in wide use now that includes games, quizzes, and review activities that students can access not only from their desktops or laptops, but also from their smartphones as well. Teachers are using this software to reinforce, summarize, and review lessons as well as to prepare students for upcoming tests.

Blended learning has developed as a natural result of using technology for learning. Blended learning involves combining or blending traditional teaching strategies with technology-based online learning. Also, some schools are using a technology-based strategy called *flipped classrooms*. In flipped classrooms, the lesson is taught through online teaching videos that students watch at home. Students then do the practice activities for the lesson the next day when they are in class.

The recent increase in online learning has resulted in the widespread use of a variety of virtual learning platforms. These platforms are designed to meet the needs of teachers to be able to create online lessons and collaborative learning spaces for their students. Many distance learning platforms also provide ways for teachers to communicate with parents. Some give teachers support through webinars, and most of the new virtual learning tools allow teachers to present interactive, multimedia lessons as well as track student progress. Schools may also utilize a combination of distance learning and in-person instruction known as a hybrid learning model.

For in-person classes, it is important to walk around the classroom to observe students as they use computers to complete their work. Help students to avoid being distracted by websites or games that are unrelated to the lesson activities. Also, monitor the use of smartphones closely. Students should not be texting or accessing social media, videos, or games if they have not completed the classwork assigned. Substitutes should help students to follow the school's established policy regarding the use of cell phones during class.

At times, students may need to charge their laptops, and this may prevent them from starting or completing the lesson activities. Locating chargers, accessing outlets, or waiting for lost Wi-Fi connections are common occurrences in today's classrooms. Technology is great when it works, but stay prepared to assist students as much as you can if it does not work. These issues can be frustrating for students, and they will need your calm resolve to help them to stay focused. Suggest that students use pen and paper if possible or work with another student. Use such moments as opportunities to demonstrate and teach patience, analytical thinking, and problem-solving. Educators refer to such times as "teaching moments," which are those times when unexpected occurrences provide the best opportunity to teach a relevant concept, principle, or idea. Table 3.4 lists just a few of the numerous devices, software, and distance learning platforms in current use.

Table 3.4 Technology in Education Popular Devices, Software, and Platforms

Devices/Hardware	Software/Platforms
Desktop computer	Schoology®
	Edmodo®
Laptop computer	Edgenuity®
	Blackboard Learn®
Chromebook®	Kahoot!®
	Canvas®
Smartboard	edpuzzle®
	edmentum®
Tablets	Khan Academy®
	Google Classroom®
Projectors	Microsoft Teams®
	Google Docs®
Cameras	Edulastic™
	Eduplanet™
Audio enhancements	Habyts™
	Skype™
Digital textbooks	Zoom™
Smartphones	

Diverse Learners

All students are entitled to an education that addresses their individual differences and special needs, including learners who are gifted as well as those who have a learning disability. According to the National Center for Education Statistics (NCES), almost 7 percent of public school students in the U.S. were classified as gifted and talented learners in a 2013 nationwide study (Digest of Education Statistics, 2013). In one state, 16 percent of the students were gifted learners. Gifted students tend to finish assignments quickly, so the challenge for teachers is to help gifted students in heterogenous groups to continue to make progress. Effective teachers prepare additional activities for their gifted students to keep them focused and engaged in learning.

The Individuals with Disabilities Education Act (IDEA) provides students between ages 3 and 21 who have disabilities with access to the most appropriate public education. Special education is sometimes referred to as *inclusion* because students with disabilities must be included with all other students in terms of their rights to a quality education. Special needs education includes a wide range of support services for students with academic, physical, cognitive, and social-emotional disabilities. Schools develop individualized education plans (IEPs) for special needs students. An IEP is a written education plan that identifies the specific types of assistance a student needs to help her/him achieve the goals of the learning program.

Also, under the U.S. Department of Education's Section 504 Regulations, special needs students are entitled to adjustments within the regular learning environment to help them achieve learning goals. These adjustments, known as *accommodations*, are alterations in the ways that classroom activities are conducted so that these students have the same opportunities for academic success as other students do. The accommodations are recorded in a student's 504 accommodations plan, and teachers can then plan the learning activities for these students accordingly. Substitute teachers do not normally have access to students' IEP and 504 records in order to protect the students' privacy and confidentiality.

English Language Learners (ELLs) are students whose native language is one other than English. ELL students may need directions and assignments translated into their native languages while they are learning to speak English. Therefore, many schools employ bilingual teachers, paraprofessionals, or instructional aides to assist ELL students in the classroom. ELL students may also have learning accommodations as well.

It is also important to note that a student's behavior may be the result of a learning disability or special need, but the best practice for substitute teachers is to refrain from any open discussion of a student's disability. Respecting and protecting the privacy and confidentiality rights of every student at all times is an important part of the job, so a student's learning pace, style, grades, or special needs should not be mentioned publicly in a classroom setting. If a student initiates a public discussion with you about grades or a disability, postpone the discussion until it can be done so privately. A staff person will initiate private discussions about a student's special needs or accommodations on a need-to-know basis for substitutes on long-term assignments. Please note the disability categories shown in Table 3.5 that are eligible for special needs education (Profiles of Students with Disabilities, 2017).

Table 3.5 Special Needs Education Categories

Disability	Description
Specific Learning Disability	Range of disorders in one or more basic psychological processes involved in language, spoken or written, that may result in impairment in ability to listen, think, read, speak, read, write, spell, or do math calculations
Speech/Language Impairment	Communication disorders such as stuttering, impaired articulation, language impairment, or voice impairment
Intellectual Disability (formerly termed "mental retardation")	Significantly subaverage general intellectual functioning
Serious Emotional Disturbance	Disability exhibiting one or more of the following characteristics over a long period of time: inability to learn, inability to sustain interpersonal relationships, inappropriate behavior/feelings, pervasive unhappiness/depression, and physical symptoms/fears related to personal/school problems
Multiple Disabilities	Concomitant impairments, the combination of which causes severe educational needs (excludes deaf-blindness)
Hearing Impairment	Impairment in hearing, permanent or fluctuating, that adversely affects educational performance and not included under the definition of deafness
Deafness	Severe hearing impairment that results in impaired processing of linguistic learning through hearing, with or without amplification, that adversely affect a child's educational performance
Orthopedic Impairment	Severe orthopedic impairment including that caused by congenital diseases, cerebral palsy, etc.
Other Health Impairments	Limitation in strength, vitality, or alertness that may be due to chronic or acute health problems such as ADD/ADHD, epilepsy, Tourette's syndrome, etc.
Visual Impairment or Blindness	Visual disability, including blindness and partial sight, adversely affecting the child's educational performance
Autism	Developmental disability significantly adversely affecting verbal and nonverbal communication and social interaction, generally evident before age 3
Traumatic Brain Injury	Acquired injury to the brain caused by external physical forces resulting in total or partial functional disability, psychosocial impairment, or both
Deaf-Blindness	Concomitant hearing and visual impairments causing severe communication and developmental and educational needs

Source: Profiles of Students with Disabilities, U.S. Department of Education, 2017

Grading

The terms *testing, grading, measurement,* and *assessment* are often used interchangeably although there are subtle differences in their meanings. The commonality among these terms is the end result, which is to obtain an objective measure of exactly how much students have learned. This section discusses the important aspects of measuring learning, including grading standards, testing methods, and types of assessments.

Learning is measured through quizzes, tests, exams, reports, projects, presentations, etc. at the end of lesson units. The data from student testing provides the basis for planning future lessons so that the students achieve course goals. The terms *goals, objectives, outcomes, benchmarks,* and *targets* are also used interchangeably to indicate the criteria for successful completion of a lesson, unit, or course. In current practice, the measure of student learning or growth has become a standard of evaluation for both students and teachers. In many places, teachers must prove that their students have shown growth. In other words, students must demonstrate that they have made measurable progress toward the established objectives. These schools use student growth objectives (SGOs) to measure learning. An SGO is a goal set by the teacher at the beginning of the course that students should be able to meet by the end of the course. Students are pretested at the start of the course and posttested at the end of the course. The pretest and posttest scores are then compared to each other to indicate if the student has shown growth by scoring higher on the posttest than s/he scored on the pretest.

In addition, grades are generally categorized as either formative or summative. The daily lesson activities and assignments within learning units generally receive formative grades. Formative grades indicate that students are cooperating during the learning process while the concept is being learned (or formed) by completing the daily assignments. Individual formative grades carry less weight than individual summative grades, and formative grading is also sometimes referred to as *low-stakes testing.* Homework assignments and quizzes are examples of low-stakes testing.

Summative grades summarize what the student has learned after the unit or course has been completed. Tests, exams, final projects, and portfolios are examples of summative grading instruments. Many summative grades are based on the A–F grading scale with a range of numerical values to earn each letter grade. A common numerical distribution for the A–F grading system is shown in Table 3.6, and this scale can vary widely among schools and districts nationally. In addition to the A–F grading scale, grading rubrics are used to determine grades. Rubrics are scoring guides that provide the criteria for evaluation, and rubrics can be used for both formative and summative

Table 3.6 Common Numerical Grade Distribution

Elementary School		Middle School		High School	
A	90–100	A +	97–100	A +	97–100
B	80–89	A	93–96	A	93–96
C	70–79	A –	90–92	A –	90–92
D	60–69	B +	87–89	B +	87–89
F	0–59	B	83–86	B	83–86
		B –	80–82	B –	80–82
		C +	77–79	C +	77–79
		C	73–76	C	73–76
		C –	70–72	C –	70–72
		D +	67–69	D +	67–69
		D	63–66	D	65–66
		D –	60–62	F	0–64
		F	0–59		

assessments. For example, English teachers frequently use rubrics to score student writing assignments such as essays, and Table 2.4 shows an example of a grading rubric that can be used to evaluate slide presentations.

Finally, the school year is divided into separate grading time frames called *marking periods*. Most K–12 schools have four marking periods per school year, and the average length of a marking period is six to eight weeks. Interim grade progress is reported about halfway through a marking period, and students receive a grade report at the end of each marking period. The final, cumulative course grade gets reported at the end of the course. Students and teachers are frequently very busy meeting the deadlines for interim grades, marking period grades, and final grades for the course. While per diem substitutes may not be required to grade assignments, long-term substitute teachers are frequently expected to grade student work, record grades, and prepare grade reports. Substitute teachers who are responsible for grading should be guided by the grading standards used in the school where they are employed.

Testing

There may be times when you will need to administer tests. Sometimes, students are nervous before or during the testing; this is known as *test anxiety*. At those times, just show them an extra measure of understanding and patience, which may help to alleviate any anxiety they may have. Classroom management procedures are covered thoroughly in Chapter 4, but there are a few differences in how a class should be conducted on test days, and those differences are noted in the next few paragraphs.

Before the Test

The lesson plan will indicate the location of the tests. Make sure there are enough test copies for the class and prevent students from accessing the test prior to testing. Take attendance and allow students time to prepare. They may need to sharpen pencils, get calculators, or change seats. Give directions for appropriate behavior during the test, including talking, cell phone use, or asking questions. Also tell students what to do when they finish. Answer preliminary questions, and make sure that everyone is settled, quiet, and ready before distributing the tests.

Distributing the Tests

Give each student one test and collect any extra copies. Note if there are different versions of the test, such as an A and B version, and distribute the tests so that adjacent students have different versions. When all tests have been distributed, count the number of students and tests so that you can confirm receipt of all tests at the end of the testing session.

During Testing

Students will usually complete tests on their own independently and silently, so maintain a quiet environment. Observe the class closely and move to different parts of the room to monitor student progress. Stay observant during interruptions while testing. Ask students to bring their tests over to you if they have a question during testing. A student should give you his/her test before leaving the room temporarily, and only allow one student out of class at a time. Let callers or visitors know that testing is in progress, and do your best to minimize distractions and unnecessary movement.

Collecting the Tests

As you collect tests, check each test for the student's name, and make sure s/he has not overlooked any portion of the test. Ask those who are finished to work on something quietly until everyone is done testing. Sometimes, a student may not be finished testing at the end of the class. If that happens, ask the student to write "Not finished" on the paper and then collect the unfinished test. Once all students have submitted their tests, count them again to confirm that all tests were collected. Place submitted tests in a secure location and prevent students from accessing the tests.

After the Test

Use your good judgment, but, in general, do not redistribute a test to a student who asks to see his/her test *well* after the testing session is over. Tell the student to check with the regular teacher when s/he returns. Once all tests have been submitted, have students proceed with the next assignment if there is time.

Electronic Testing

If students will be completing a test online on a desktop or laptop, take attendance first and ensure that everyone is ready before the test starts. Minimize distractions and unnecessary movement, and maintain a quiet environment. Go over to a student if s/he has a question or technology issue. Monitor progress and make sure students have only the test window open on the screen. Remind students to follow the proper procedure for saving the test online. Ask those who are finished to work quietly (offline) until everyone is done. Ensure that all tests have been completed and all test screens are closed before proceeding with other activities.

Standardized Assessment

Standardized assessment refers to the wide variety of methods and tools that educators use to evaluate, measure, and document the academic readiness, learning progress, skill acquisition, or educational needs of students. The standards for course content have been developed at the national level, including the core group of competencies that all students should master within each of the major subject areas. This core group of competencies and their corresponding standards are known as the Common Core. The Common Core was developed as a national standard to be implemented in every state so that the students in every state are held to the same standard (thus having those standards in common). Although, the Common Core was initially proposed as a national standard to be implemented in every state, some states chose not to adopt the Common Core standards but opted for their own standards instead.

State tests that are administered to public school students annually measure their achievement levels based on the Common Core standards. Teaching, curriculum development, and testing and measurement may all be guided by Common Core standards. Teachers are frequently required to align lesson goals and instruction with Common Core standards and to indicate that alignment in their lesson plans. Public schools receive "report cards" based on their students' scores on the state's standardized tests, their results are reported to the public, and schools can then be rated in comparison to each other. The Every Student Succeeds Act (ESSA) now governs K–12 public education in the U.S. (Every Student Succeeds Act, 2015).

Finally, the Preliminary Scholastic Achievement Test (PSAT), Scholastic Achievement Test (SAT), and the American College Test (ACT) are standardized assessments that are administered to determine a student's probability of academic success in college. These college entrance examinations may also be given in high schools at various times during the school year. Students usually take the PSAT once in grade 10 or 11. Students may take the SAT anytime starting in grade 9, but most students take the SAT in grade 11 and/or 12. Both the SAT and ACT are currently administered seven times a year. Substitute teachers will not typically be involved in administering the college entrance exams, but they may need to substitute for teachers on the days when these exams are scheduled in schools. Table 3.7 summarizes the common types of assessments.

Table 3.7 Common Types of Assessments

Type of Assessment	Description	Example
Diagnostic	Collects data on a student's knowledge before instruction	Pretest
Formative	Monitors student learning during the learning process	Worksheet to complete after reading/discussion
Benchmark	Measures whether learning goals have been reached at the end of a unit of study	Test, quiz, report
Summative	Measures whether learning outcomes have been reached at the end of the course or unit	Test, quiz, exam
Norm-referenced	Measures student performance against an average norm (compares student to other students)	PSAT, SAT, ACT
Criterion-referenced	Measures student performance against a set standard of criteria	Standardized state test

References

32 Research-Based Instructional Strategies. 2020, February 3. Retrieved April 15, 2020, from teachthought.com/pedagogy/32-research-based-instructional-strategies/.

Every Student Succeeds Act (ESSA). 2015. U.S. Department of Education. Retrieved April 4, 2020, from ed.gov/policy/elsec/leg/essa.

Kagan, S. and M. Kagan. 2013. *Kagan Cooperative Learning*. Kagan Publishing. San Clemente, CA.

Profiles of Students with Disabilities. U.S. Department of Education. 2017, May 2. Retrieved April 25, 2020, from ed.gov/idea/regs//a/300.8.

U.S. Department of Education, National Center for Education Statistics (NCES), Digest of Education Statistics. 2013. Retrieved June 24, 2020, from nces.ed.gov./programs/digest/d17.

4

Classroom Management

The Importance of Classroom Management

Effective classroom management includes implementing procedures for getting class started, distributing/collecting materials, keeping students on task, and managing interruptions and behavior. Effective teachers have routines that minimize wasted time and resources, and the lesson plan may indicate the daily routines. Smaller classes may provide fewer management challenges than larger classes, but classroom management skills are very important regardless of the number of students in a class. Teachers are also evaluated on their ability to manage the classroom environment in a way that facilitates learning for all students. This chapter highlights the most important elements of effective classroom management.

Getting Class Started

Substitute and interim teachers, please remember this critically important rule when working in a school: **Never leave your students unattended**. Arrive in the classroom before the students because in most places you are prohibited from leaving students unattended for *any* length of time. If an emergency arises that requires you to leave a classroom full of students, contact the office and wait for another staff member to arrive.

Establishing Order and Getting the Students' Attention

Getting the class off to a good start includes getting the class quiet and attentive, recording attendance, distributing handouts/supplies, explaining the lesson, and getting the students engaged in the lesson activities. Try to arrive at the classroom before the students to become familiar with the lesson plan, attendance list, fire drill procedure, etc. Locate key items like the hall passes, textbooks, and other supplies. Many teachers have the agenda and essential question for the lesson displayed on the board. The agenda lists the day's tasks in their order of completion, and the essential question (EQ) is related to the topic being studied that students should be able to answer at the end of the unit. Print your name clearly on the board if possible. Some schools also require teachers to stand at their classroom doors to help monitor the hallways as students arrive.

Follow the school's procedure when it is time to start class. Some schools require classroom doors to be closed and locked when the late bell rings. Get the students' attention immediately. If the class is very noisy, develop a way to get the students' attention without yelling. Effective methods for getting students quiet and gaining their attention include:

- ◆ Ringing a bell
- ◆ Flicking the lights off and on
- ◆ Saying, "Attention, everyone, quiet please."
- ◆ Saying, "Everyone stop talking, please, and thanks for not talking while I'm talking."
- ◆ Doing a countdown saying, "I need quiet in 5, 4, 3, 2, 1."
- ◆ Saying, "Clap once, if you hear me." "Clap twice."
- ◆ Raising your hand without speaking. Students will begin to stop talking and also raise their hands in response to your raised hand. Continue until everyone is quiet.

Introduce yourself and set a positive tone. Establish your authority in a calm, confident, and respectful way. Briefly explain the behavior expected regarding noise level, asking questions, moving around the room, etc. Getting started efficiently is a large part of good classroom management.

Distribute Handouts and Supplies

Distribute the handouts that students will need to complete the lesson as quickly and efficiently as possible. Students may need to retrieve textbooks, pens, paper, laptops, or other supplies in addition to any handouts for the lesson. Streamline this process, asking students to retrieve supplies as quickly and quietly as possible within three to five minutes or less. Sometimes, high school classes have a student aide who has been assigned to assist the teacher. If so, allow the student aide to assist as needed.

Give the Lesson Directions

Once the handouts/supplies are distributed and students are quiet, announce the directions from the teacher's lesson plan. Read the directions aloud clearly. If the plan includes several activities, you could use a teaching technique known as *chunking* to present the activities a few at a time so that students do not become confused with too many directions all at once. For example, if the lesson includes five activities, say, "There are five total activities to do, and I will explain the first three now and give you the last two in a few minutes." Answer general questions regarding the lesson for the class as a whole. Let those who understand get started and address any remaining questions individually. After attendance is recorded, double-check the lesson plan to make sure you have given students all of the directions. If there is available board space, it is a good idea to write directions on a whiteboard or chalkboard, especially if the plan includes several activities so that students know everything they need to accomplish. It is best, however, to avoid using the smartboard unless you have authorized access to the school's computer system and have also completed smartboard training.

Recording Attendance

The recording and retention of student attendance records is mandated by state laws in the U.S., so it is important that attendance be recorded promptly, neatly, and accurately. You may want to give the class the lesson assignment first and then take attendance as close to the start of class as possible. Many times, there will be a computer printout of the class or an attendance book to use for recording attendance such as the one illustrated in Figure 4.1. In addition, some of the codes commonly used to record attendance are shown in Table 4.1.

TEACHER _____ **CLASS PERIOD** _____ **DATE** _____

STUDENT	P	T	A

Figure 4.1 Student Attendance Form

Table 4.1 Attendance Codes

P	Present
Dot or check mark	Present
A	Absent
T	Tardy/Late
TU	Tardy/Late Unexcused (no note or pass)
TE	Tardy/Late Excused (had note or pass)
ED	Early Dismissal (also record the time)

Learn the students' names also because class management becomes much easier when you can identify students by name. An effective technique for learning students' names quickly is to take a sign-in sheet around the room in a specific order. Ask students to *print their names clearly* as you walk down the rows from front to back or around the tables clockwise. Repeat in the same order for each row or table. In that way, you can identify and address students by name from this sheet. Using this method takes a little longer than simply calling names, but students control their behavior better for substitute teachers who know their names. You can use this procedure even when there is an attendance book or computer printout. Just transfer attendance to the book or printout at some point during the class. If there is no attendance book or printout available, then your print-in sheet is the official attendance record.

Teachers often assign seats to maximize learning for each student, and, if so, they create diagrams or seat charts that show the seating arrangement for the class. Teachers usually leave their seat charts in the substitute teacher folder with the lesson plans, and students should be required to sit in their assigned seats. Ask students to move to their assigned seats before you take attendance to facilitate classroom management. However, avoid using the seat chart to record attendance unless explicitly instructed to do so. The attendance book, computer printout, or printed sign-in sheet is the authorized attendance record. Sometimes, schools require the class attendance be sent to the office. If so, send the student aide or a reliable student to deliver the attendance to the appropriate office. The regular teacher and/or the attendance officer is responsible for the official daily attendance records, which are usually recorded electronically. The long-term substitutes may have access to the computer system to record attendance electronically, but per diem substitutes will usually record student attendance on a paper form similar to the one shown in Figure 4.1.

Getting Students Engaged in the Lesson Activities

After the attendance has been taken and the lesson directions have been given, circulate around the class to monitor, encourage, and assist students with the lesson. Make sure that each student is working on the assigned lesson. Double-check the lesson plan to make sure that students have the entire assignment. When every student is working, continue to monitor the class and maintain a generally quiet and orderly environment which will help the students to complete the day's assignment(s) successfully.

Maintaining the Learning Environment

While the class is in session and the students are engaged in learning, maintaining the learning environment involves maximizing student time on task by minimizing distractions and handling interruptions effectively. The goal is to help students to focus with as few disruptions to the learning process as possible. For this reason, schools try to limit movement in and out of classrooms while classes are in session. Even so, there are times when interruptions may occur, and effective teachers know how to minimize their distracting effects. This section outlines some common causes of class interruptions and the most efficient ways to manage them.

Students Arriving Late

Students should have a late pass or some other type of authorization to enter class late, but permit students to enter late with or without a pass as long as their names are on the class list (unless school policy says otherwise). Demonstrate patience if students arrive late, and avoid making comments or asking questions concerning their lateness. Try to keep latecomers from distracting the other students, and help them to get started as quietly and unobtrusively as possible. Monitor late students until they are on task and working on the lesson activities. Remember to record attendance for late students.

Restroom and Nurse

Schools have established guidelines for allowing students to leave the room while the class is in session. During the class, students may be allowed to go to the restroom or nurse, but this process must be managed very carefully. Elementary schools may require a staff person to escort students when classes are in session. Middle and high school students may be permitted to leave the room with written or electronic authorization such as a hall pass. Some schools do not permit students to leave the room for any reason during the first ten minutes and the last ten minutes of class. Determine the school's policy as soon as possible upon arrival and follow the established policy consistently. Since it is the substitute teacher's responsibility to keep track of every student present, the following guidelines are recommended:

◆ Maintain control of students leaving the room during class but respect their personal right to go the restroom or the nurse (especially if a student says it's an emergency).
◆ Permit only one student to leave the room at a time; students should not leave in groups.
◆ Issue each student a written or electronic hall pass. A written hall pass should include the student's name, date, time, destination, and your signature. Students should have the written pass when they return. Some schools require that students receive a written pass, sign out before leaving, and sign in upon return. If so, make sure

students sign their name, destination, time left, and time of return. An electronic hall pass will require you to enter a class code to indicate your approval when they leave. You enter the code again when they return. Look for this code on the teacher's lesson plan and note the student's name and time left.

◆ Minimize students going to other classrooms, the library, etc., unless the lesson plan indicates otherwise (especially if the student has not completed the assigned work).

◆ Do not allow students to visit or stay in your class if their name is not on the class attendance list.

◆ Notify the appropriate office of students who have an early dismissal, leave without permission, or leave with permission but do not return.

◆ Do not deviate from the school's established policy.

Early Dismissals

There are times when a student may be excused to leave class/school early for medical appointments, sports games, etc. It is important to confirm the student's early dismissal by calling the appropriate school office before dismissing the student. Early dismissals for sports team members may be announced via the public address system. The school office may also send a staff person to escort elementary students with early dismissals. To ensure student safety, confirm that all early dismissals are officially authorized.

Incoming Calls on Classroom Phone

The main office, nurse, counselor, or another teacher may call the classroom for a student. When answering, identify the room the caller has reached and then identify yourself. Note the caller's name and send the student promptly, making note of the student's name, the time, and his/her destination. You may still need to issue the student a hall pass and have him/her sign out as well. Avoid using the school telephones for personal calls.

Practice Drills

Schools are required to conduct practice drills for emergency situations, such as fire drills, lockdown drills, and shelter-in-place drills. Stay prepared for these practice drills by keeping the emergency procedures readily accessible and familiarizing yourself with those procedures. For fire drills, have the students exit in an orderly manner. Follow the school's policy to either remain with the same class or join a different class. Attendance must be taken at the outside destination so that all students are accounted for. When the drill ends and the students return to class, verify the attendance once again. Then try to get the students back on task as quickly as possible although it may take them a few minutes to settle down after a drill. Chapter 5 details additional information on practice drills and emergency preparedness.

Classroom Visitors

Administrators and other staff may enter a room while a class is in session. Administrators may come in to check on the class in the teacher's absence, or other staff may come in to distribute items, see a student, etc. Whatever the reason for the visit, the class will be temporarily distracted, so do your best to get them to stay focused on the lesson as you handle visitors to the class. Any visitors from outside the school should be authorized by the main office and be wearing a visitor's badge.

Managing Behavior

The daily pressures of school can be a bit much at times, which is why students are sometimes relieved to have a substitute teacher for the day. For middle and high school students especially, their "misbehavior" could simply be an expression of their relief from the pressures of the regular routine. Elementary students may need a moment to adjust to your presence. A substitute teacher is a stranger to younger children, so they may need time to realize that they are safe with you. Keep in mind that misbehavior, if any, is not personal. Usually, students will settle down once they adjust to the fact that they have a substitute for the day, so give them a few minutes. An older student may challenge your authority. If that happens, respectfully clarify that each student must control his/her behavior according to the school's code of conduct. Students will eventually cooperate when you politely insist on appropriate behavior.

Each class or group of students is different and subject to the principles of group dynamics. That is why some classes may seem quieter, more attentive, or more noisy than others. The expectations and management techniques of the regular teacher also influence the group dynamics of a class. Classes whose teachers use a laissez-faire management style have a different dynamic from those classes whose teachers use a more authoritative management style. Having a basic understanding of group dynamics and the different management styles will help you to understand how to successfully manage groups of students.

It is also helpful to remember that there are times when occurrences in school or outside of school make it very difficult for students to manage their own behavior. Students tend to be excited at certain times more than others, and this may be reflected in their behavior, the class noise level, etc. An extra measure of patience is needed at these times. Take note of the times in the following paragraphs when student behavior might be affected by external events.

Weekends and Holidays

Students tend to be excited on Fridays and days preceding and following a holiday or break. The class may be more noisy than usual. Simply acknowledge the students' excitement (and maybe yours too), but let them know that the classwork must go on nonetheless. Of course, do not allow any unsafe behavior, but just realize that at these times their behavior, for the most part, is only a reflection of their excitement.

School Events

Students also get revved up near special school events such as prom, pep rally, a big game, field day, spirit week, picture day, the school play, the choir concert, the first or last day of school, birthdays, and graduation. Be gracious and patient during these times and enjoy the atmosphere of celebration.

Practice Drills

It generally takes students a few minutes to settle down after an emergency practice drill, and this is also to be expected. Do your best to get them refocused on the lesson. They will usually settle down before too long.

Grade Reports

Sometimes, students may be anxious or excited at or near the times that grade reports are released. The deadlines for submitting assignments at the end of the marking periods can cause stress for many students. In addition, they may be excited about a good grade or disappointed with a not-so-good grade. It is common for students to express their feelings at these times and also for their behavior to reflect those feelings.

Bereavement (Loss of Student/Staff)

The times of the loss of another student or staff person are difficult moments in schools, and teachers have to be especially compassionate at those times. If a loss is announced during your class, students may need time to process the news. Demonstrate patience and empathy. Some students may not have a reaction at all, but it is perfectly fine to allow some time to express their feelings if they need to. If a student seems overcome with strong emotions, s/he may need to speak to a counselor or the school psychologist. Many times, schools have a planned procedure for times of school bereavement with a crisis team in place to assist.

Current Events

Students are affected by current events as well, whether they are positive or negative. Lessons will be interrupted and students will be distracted when major current events happen locally, nationally, or globally. Allow time for expression before, during, or after the planned lesson activities, and remain neutral as much as possible regarding controversial current events.

Personal Events

Students will at times be affected by occurrences in their own lives, and they may be uncooperative for personal reasons. The student may be experiencing health issues. The illness or loss of a family member, friend, or even a pet will probably impact student behavior. Other issues with family, friends, social media, etc. could affect a student's attitude and behavior. There are actually times when the best thing to do is permit a student to postpone doing the assignment. The best practice for teachers is to exercise an abundance of caution when working with a student who continues to resist their attempts to get him or her engaged in the lesson activities.

Cyberbullying/Social Media

Sometimes, a student may be distracted and/or upset by a text message or a social media post. The student loses focus on the lesson and may express the issue openly for others to hear. Stay alert for any signs of bullying or cyberbullying, which could be a serious problem. Do your best to try to help the student to refocus on the lesson. Also, try to prevent students from texting or making social media posts during their class time with you. You do not need to be held accountable for anything that might be inappropriately posted at a time that the student was in class with you. If you suspect bullying behavior or if the student does not refocus after some time, quietly ask the student if s/he needs to see the counselor. Teenagers in particular can sometimes get caught up in their social interactions, and it may not turn out to be serious at all. But, it might still be advisable to alert a counselor, the dean, or another teacher at some point. In that way, you have done your job to guard and protect student safety.

Learning Disabilities

Students with certain types of learning disabilities sometimes exhibit disruptive behavior. Those who are diagnosed with social and/or emotional disabilities sometimes have difficulty focusing on the lesson at hand. A student may seem uncooperative or defiant, which could signal an underlying disability. At times, a student's misbehavior is masking a learning disability and the student is "acting out" to cover up the fact that s/he has a problem—for example, with reading comprehension. Never take a student's misbehavior personally. Remain objective and keep in mind that some students express their learning frustrations in ways that could be interpreted as misbehavior.

School Emergencies

Any kind of real emergency will require the suspension of normal activities. Actual fires, as well as weather-related or other emergencies, cause unavoidable disruption. Be guided by the school's emergency protocols as well as common sense when managing student behavior before, during, and after any real school emergency.

In general, in order to prevent or minimize student misbehavior, teach the entire class the behavioral expectations so that everyone is informed. For example, explain to the entire class that an acceptable noise level results when every person keeps his/her voice volume slightly above a whisper. Start with objective explanations to the whole group and follow up with respectful reminders to individual students if needed. Emphasize to the students that you are there to help them learn and that you are their advocate—not their enemy. You could mention that those who practice self-discipline do not need discipline from others.

If misbehavior interferes with other learners, try to speak quietly with the student in a nonconfrontational way. Students will often change bad behavior if you speak with them individually without the class as their audience. Students generally want to trust and respect you. As always, respect is earned and reciprocal, so maintain a respectful tone and model respectful behavior even when handling misbehavior. Stay calm and avoid engaging in power struggles or confrontations with students. Refer to the student code of conduct handbook that most schools provide to outline acceptable behavior. Also, note the list of suggested teacher responses shown in Table 4.2 that are designed to effectively manage student behavior.

If misbehavior or disruption persists, document the behavior and the action you took. A written record may be needed later, and documenting misbehavior also helps teachers to remain patient and professional. Using a form like the sample behavior log shown in Figure 4.2, note the student's name, date, time, description of the behavior, and the action you took. Notify the offender(s) of your intent to call the office if the misbehavior continues. Students may stop bad behavior if they know you are serious about reporting them.

If you think the situation warrants it after you have documented misbehavior and also given ample warning of your intent to contact the office, call for discipline assistance. It is better to be overly cautious by calling for help rather than to allow a situation to escalate out of control. If necessary, seek assistance from a nearby staff member until the designated help arrives. In general, take verbal or physical threats, physical aggression, or bullying behavior seriously. In fact, schools everywhere have launched programs to raise awareness concerning the seriousness of bullying. All forms of bullying, including cyberbullying, are now considered to be major discipline infractions. There may also be a school resource officer available to safely resolve any serious discipline issues. **As always, avoid physically touching students.**

Finally, my general policy has been to include any serious discipline issues in the report I leave for the regular teacher. In my opinion, it is best to allow the regular teacher to make the decision about how to follow up on any student misbehavior during his/her absence. For that reason, I try to avoid preparing and submitting official disciplinary paperwork to the school discipline staff (unless I am explicitly instructed to do so). I leave the decision to the regular teacher and/or discipline staff concerning assigning detentions, suspensions, or other kinds of formal disciplinary measures. Of course, follow the guidelines in place at your particular schools. Table 4.3 outlines a few helpful examples of how to successfully manage student behavior and includes results that I have experienced when implementing the suggested solution.

Table 4.2 Suggested Teacher Responses for Managing Student Behavior

General Methods of Gaining Cooperation
Communicate the expected behavior to the entire class.
Praise any cooperative behaviors you observe.
Make polite requests to the entire class.
Remind the class of expectations.
Stand near a disruptive student.
Speak to a disruptive student quietly.
Call a nearby teacher for help (a disruptive student may work better in a familiar teacher's room).

Statements to Reinforce/Encourage Great Behavior
"So far, so good, class. Please keep it up."
"Thanks for staying quiet and focused."
"I think I can leave a good report for this class."
"You're doing well—keep it up."
"This is a great class."

Statements to Redirect Students (Help Them Regain/Retain Focus)
"Stay focused, please."
"Lower your voices, please."
"Quiet, please."
"Thanks for staying quiet, everyone."
"No off-task conversation until you've finished, please."
"Phones away, please."
"Don't let your phone distract you."
"Please stay respectful."
"Please maintain (or regain) self-control."
Any positive comments related to the lesson

Examples of What You Should Never Say to a Class or Student
Any type of name-calling/ridiculing
Any type of sarcasm
Excessively authoritative comments
Empty threats or warnings
References to appearance
Disrespect of any kind
Yelling/screaming
Profanity
References to a student's special education needs
The words "stupid, idiot, retarded"
The direction to a student or class to "shut up"
Negative labels such as "bad," "awful," etc.

Student	Date/Time/Description	Action Taken
John Doe	3/12/19, Period 3, 12:30 p.m., loud and disruptive off-task conversation	Redirected him more than three times

Figure 4.2 Sample Behavior Log

Table 4.3 Managing Student Behavior

Behavior	Suggested Solution	Result
Students calling out, causing class disruption	Politely remind the students to stop calling out and to raise hands for questions.	May take more than one reminder. Most settled down but had to speak privately with offenders on many occasions.
Student on phone, ignoring class assignment	Explain that checking phone periodically is OK and make polite request to start the assignment.	May take more than one request. Most complied, but I've let it go for a few who stayed on their phones after many requests but were not disruptive.
Students having disruptive off-task conversation	Make polite request to lower voices and minimize off-task conversation.	May take more than one request. Most have complied when I persist. Some kept talking with much lower voices—I let it go a few times if they weren't disruptive.
Student has head down with incomplete classwork	Ask student if s/he is ill. Send to nurse, if yes. If not, make polite request to complete work.	Many complied, but for those few who kept their heads down, I noted it for the teacher.
Student does not return or walks out without permission	Note time the student left and notify office.	In some instances, student returned; in others, student never returned to class. Noted it for the teacher.
Students throwing objects (pens, water bottles, etc.)	Tell students not to throw things. Repeat the reminder if needed.	Most times, nothing else was thrown; have had to repeat reminder, warn students who defied, and report those who persisted to the discipline office.

Student visibly upset (crying)	Ask student if s/he would like to go to nurse or counselor (or restroom). Quietly acknowledge that you see student is upset; do not pry.	Have had students who went to restroom/counselor or stayed and calmed down.
Students hitting, chasing, having physical interaction	Instruct students to stop and be seated; state that physical interaction is not permitted.	Stopped when I stood near students. Have had to warn to call disciplinarian.
Students copying each other's work	Ask students to do the assignment without copying from others. Repeat the request as needed.	Some have gotten away with this. The challenge is that this seems to be acceptable in some schools.
Student texting to receive answers during test	Notify the team teacher who is present.	Team teacher who was in charge ignored it. I would have instructed students to stop texting had I been in charge.
Student using profanity, name-calling, bullying	Politely request to the student to refrain from the behavior. Repeat as needed.	Sometimes, behavior persisted. Have had to warn students of referral to disciplinarian. Have also noted behavior for teacher.

Dismissal Procedures

Class Dismissal

Ending a class efficiently involves making sure that students have identified and submitted their assignments, replaced all supplies, discarded trash, etc. Note the guidelines below for ending every class efficiently.

- Give yourself and the class enough time to finish in an organized way by announcing the lesson closure five to ten minutes before the end of class.
- If students are submitting papers, make sure their names are on their papers as they are being submitted.
- Organize submitted classwork neatly—attach a note with the date, class, etc. Clip together and stack neatly on teacher's desk.
- Require students to restack books, replace supplies, remove trash, push in chairs, etc.
- Students should remain at or near their seats until dismissed.
- Monitor the door, and do not allow students to leave before the ending class bell.
- Thank the students for cooperating or wish them a good day.

School Dismissal

Ending the school day efficiently is just as important as getting the day off to a good start. At the end of the school day, use the same procedure you followed at the end of class, but dismissal procedures vary among elementary, middle, and high schools. Elementary and/or middle school teachers may be required to walk students to their buses or some other outside location and see that they board buses safely. Remember that you are responsible for the students under your supervision until they are safely and officially released from your care. If necessary, return to the classroom to ensure that things are in order as stated earlier. A successful day results from doing your best from the first bell to the last bell, so stay focused even after the students have been dismissed to ensure that you have a strong finish to what was hopefully a successful school day.

Some additional tips for a strong finish include:

- Follow the same procedure outlined above for ending a class efficiently.
- Leave your comments/feedback concerning the day on the teacher's desk using a form like the one shown in Figure 4.3.
- Stay until the official dismissal time for substitute staff.

- ◆ Remember to gather all your belongings.
- ◆ Turn off lights; close and lock the classroom door.
- ◆ Proceed to the office and follow the exit procedure. Return classroom keys and badges, and sign out if required.
- ◆ Let the office staff know you're leaving, and exit the school grounds promptly.
- ◆ Maintain professionalism at all times, including while you are leaving the school property. Unless a student is your relative, do not give students rides.
- ◆ Use a form like the one shown in Figure 4.4 to evaluate your performance in accordance with reflective practice (reflect on your successes or plans for improvement).

SAMPLE SUBSTITUTE TEACHER REPORT

TEACHER _____   DATE _____

Period 1:   Went well. Students completed assigned work with no major issues.

Period 2:   Fire drill in beginning. Students took a few minutes to refocus upon returning. No major issues.

Period 3:   A few students had trouble accessing the assignment online. Mr. Jones (next-door teacher) assisted and remainder of class went well.

Period 4:   Most students worked well. I had to redirect behavior at Table 4 (at least three times)—slightly disrespectful but they eventually settled down. They did not complete the assignment during class.

Comments: It was good day overall—thank you.

_____Mrs. Doe_____
Substitute Teacher's Signature

Figure 4.3 Sample Substitute Teacher Report

REFLECTIVE PRACTICE SELF-EVALUATION FORM

DATE _____   **SCHOOL**_____

TEACHER _____   **SUBJECT(S)**_____

Directions: Rate yourself on a scale from 1 (poor) to 5 (proficient). Include comments for future reference.

PROFESSIONALISM

Punctuality   1 2 3 4 5   _____

Appearance   1 2 3 4 5   _____

Attitude   1 2 3 4 5   _____

Interactions with staff   1 2 3 4 5   _____

Interactions with students   1 2 3 4 5   _____

CLASS MANAGEMENT

Reviewed lesson plans   1 2 3 4 5   _____

Reviewed emergency procedures   1 2 3 4 5   _____

Took attendance promptly   1 2 3 4 5   _____

Learned students' names   1 2 3 4 5   _____

Efficiently executed lesson plan   1 2 3 4 5   _____

Answered questions thoroughly   1 2 3 4 5   _____

Kept students engaged in learning 1 2 3 4 5   _____

Handled student movement
   in/out of room efficiently   1 2 3 4 5   _____

Handled disruptions / behavior
   issues effectively   1 2 3 4 5   _____

Ended class sessions effectively
   (room in order, etc.)   1 2 3 4 5   _____

OVERALL RATING   1 2 3 4 5   _____

Figure 4.4 Reflective Practice Self-Evaluation Form

5

School Safety

- The Importance of School Safety
- General Overview

The Importance of School Safety

In the years since Columbine, school safety and security has entered a new dimension of awareness and preparedness training. It is a vitally important part of the substitute teacher's responsibility to know the emergency procedures for each building and classroom to which s/he is assigned and to protect the safety and security of every student. The substitute teacher's assignment includes guarding children's lives, so your alertness and preparedness is crucial.

This chapter does not provide comprehensive or explicit details on the many facets of school emergency preparedness with which you must become familiar. Rather, this is an overview with general information only. The actual, specific emergency procedures for you to follow will be provided to you at your individual schools. Take the initiative to get all of the emergency preparedness information and training that you will need to be qualified to work in schools and to protect the safety and well-being of each and every one of your students.

General Overview

Determine your school's specific procedures as soon as possible upon your arrival, and always refer to the schools' specific guidelines for emergency procedures and protocols. Your own preparedness could impact the safety of students, so the importance of you being informed and prepared cannot be overemphasized. In many schools, teachers are required to keep emergency information in an emergency folder that is easy to identify and readily accessible by the substitute teacher. The lesson plan may indicate the location of the emergency folder, which should contain the following information:

◆ Emergency procedures for fire drills, lockdown drills, shelter-in-place drills, etc.
◆ Phone numbers of key staff, such as main office, nurse, dean, etc.
◆ Attendance lists
◆ Teacher's schedule
◆ Staff/faculty phone directory
◆ Map of school
◆ Names of helpful staff
◆ Health concerns of specific students

Fire Drills

In many places, state law requires that schools conduct fire drills once a month. The route a class takes during a fire drill should be in the emergency folder and sometimes will also be posted near the classroom door. Upon arrival in your classroom, determine the fire drill route, destination, and attendance procedure. At the fire drill alarm, see that every student exits the room in an orderly manner, and proceed immediately to the established destination outside of the building. Follow the procedure for recording/reporting student attendance. Wait for the all-clear signal before reentering the building. Upon return to the class, confirm class attendance.

Lockdown Drills

Schools are also now required to perform lockdown drills to practice preparedness in the event of an intruder within the school or the nearby community. During a lockdown drill, classroom doors and windows must be closed and locked. Everyone should move away from any windows, and the windows should be covered. Silence should be maintained throughout the duration of the drill. The school safety team may check that all doors are locked and that the room is silent. Demonstrate a calm resolve to help students feel safe in your care. Wait for the all-clear signal before resuming normal class activity.

Shelter-in-Place Drills

Shelter-in-place procedures are also conducted periodically to practice preparedness for weather-related events. During shelter-in-place drills in some schools, doors are locked and students must remain in the classroom away from windows. In other places, shelter in place requires movement to inside hallways or other areas away from any windows. An all-clear signal will be given at the end of the drill.

Other Types of Emergency Preparedness

There are other types of emergency practices that schools conduct to ensure the preparedness of students and staff. Evacuation drills are important in the case of bomb threats, gas leaks, or other events requiring building evacuation. In these instances, the procedure may be similar to a fire drill except for the destination outside of the building. Emergency preparedness training is now provided routinely to school staff, and, in many places, the staff is required to complete online training, attend training workshops, and/or obtain completion certificates to show preparedness for a variety of school emergencies.

Table 5.1 Emergency Actions and Responses

Emergency Actions

All Clear	Take Cover
Emergency Damage Assessment	Duck, Cover, and Hold On
Lockdown	Evacuation
Secure Campus	Off-Site Evacuation
Shelter in Place	Structured Reunification

Emergency Responses

Active Shooter / Armed Assailant	Gas Odor/Leak
Aircraft Accident	Intruder
Air Pollution Alert	Irrational Behavior
Allergic Reaction	Kidnapping
Animal Disturbance	Medical Emergency
Biological Agent Release	Missing Student
Bomb Threat	Motor Vehicle Accident
Bus Accident	Pandemic (Influenza)
Chemical Accident (off-site)	Poisoning/Contamination
Chemical Accident (on-site)	Public Demonstration
Civil Disobedience	Sexual Assault
Death of a Student	Student Riot
Dirty Bomb	Suicide Attempt
Earthquake	Suspicious Package
Explosion	Threat/Assault
Fire (off-site)	Utility Failure
Fire (on-site)	War / Terrorist Attack
Flood	Weather-Related Emergency

Source: Multihazard Emergency Planning for Schools Toolkit, FEMA, 2011

Table 5.2 Threat and Hazard Types and Examples

Threat and Hazard Type	Examples
Natural Hazards	• Earthquakes • Tornadoes • Lightning • Severe wind • Hurricanes • Floods • Wildfires • Extreme temperatures • Landslides or mudslides • Tsunamis • Volcanic eruptions • Winter precipitation
Technological Hazards	• Explosions or accidental release of toxins from industrial plants • Accidental release of hazardous materials from within the school, such as gas leaks or laboratory spills • Hazardous materials releases from major highways or railroads • Radiological releases from nuclear power stations • Dam failure • Power failure • Water failure
Biological Hazards	• Infectious diseases such as pandemic influenza, extensively drug-resistant tuberculosis, *Staphylococcus aureus*, and meningitis • Contaminated food outbreaks, including salmonella, botulism, and *E. coli* • Toxic materials present in school laboratories
Adversarial, Incidental, and Human-Caused Threats	• Fire • Active shooters • Criminal threats or actions • Gang violence • Bomb threats • Domestic violence and abuse • Cyber attacks • Suicide

Source: Threat and Hazard Types and Examples, REMS K–12 Guide, U.S. Department of Education, 2013

There is a wealth of information available in the Multihazard Emergency Planning for Schools Toolkit on the Federal Emergency Management Agency (FEMA) website at fema.gov. FEMA provides training materials, hazard analysis, prevention and preparedness, and procedures/protocols. In addition, the Resources for Emergency Management in Schools (REMS) Toolkit on the U.S. Department of Education website (ed.gov) is another reliable resource that provides comprehensive information for managing school emergencies. Each school or district is responsible for developing emergency preparedness operations for all of its buildings and providing the necessary training to its teachers and other staff. Many schools and districts use the ALICE Training system (ALICE Training, 2016). ALICE is an acronym for Alert, Lockdown, Inform, Counter, Evacuate, and the ALICE system includes emergency training for schools and other organizations through webinars, speakers, and videos. **Again, always be sure to locate and become familiar with the emergency procedures and protocols that are specific to your school.** Table 5.1 outlines general emergency actions and responses, and Table 5.2 illustrates some of the most common threats and hazards.

References

ALICE Training, A Solution of Navigate 360. 2016. Retrieved June 25, 2020, from Alicetraining.com/training-options.

Multihazard Emergency Planning for Schools Toolkit. Federal Emergency Management Agency (FEMA). 2011, March. Retrieved April 30, 2020, from training.fema.gov/programs/emischool/el361toolkit.

Threat and Hazard Types and Examples. U.S. Department of Education. Resources for Emergency Management in Schools. REMS K-12 Guide, page 36. 2013, June. Retrieved June 2, 2020, from rems.ed.gov/docs/REMS_K-12_Guide_508.pdf.

Closing Thoughts

I hope this handbook has been helpful in some way, and I just wanted to close with a few words of encouragement to each one of you. I have enjoyed a successful career as a classroom teacher, and I am now also enjoying substituting during my retirement years. To me, substitute teaching is one of the most interesting part-time jobs that anyone could have. Children are full of life, laughter, and hope, which is contagious and invigorating. On one of my best days ever as a substitute teacher, I introduced myself to the class as usual, saying: "Good morning, everybody. I'm Mrs. Washington." I will always cherish the moment when the dark-haired, third-grade boy called out enthusiastically from his seat: "Are you George Washington's wife?" Now *that* was a really good day! I wish you those types of really good days and happy memories in the weeks, months, and years to come.

Of course, there might be a day here or there that challenges your strength, and, yes, I have had those as well. A challenging day I remember the most was the day that I was locked down in a classroom with 20 high schoolers for more than two hours because of an incident in the neighborhood not far from the school. The students were all lying or sitting on the floor near or under tables and chairs. I was seated on a chair near them, and at one point I stood up to shift my position. I will never forget the fear that I heard in the teenage girl's voice when she pleaded with me tearfully, "Ms. Washington, get down!" The lockdown finally ended, and thankfully we were all OK. Those students and I never forgot that day. It was the day we became true friends.

In closing, thank you again for doing such important work. May your good days far outweigh your challenging days. My hope and my prayer is that somehow you'll enjoy them all!

Your colleague and friend, Barbara Washington

Recommended Resources

ALICE Training Portal. Retrieved from Alicetraining.com/training-options/individual-certification.

Beckett, Chris and Hillary Taylor. 2019. *Human Growth and Development*, 4th Edition. Sage Publications. Thousand Oaks, CA.

Burke, Kay. 2008. *What to Do with The Kid Who . . . Developing Cooperation, Self-Discipline, and Responsibility in the Classroom*, 3rd Edition. Corwin Press, Sage Publications. Thousand Oaks, CA.

Curwin, Richard, Allen Mendler and Brian Mendler. 2018. *Discipline with Dignity, 4th Edition: How to Build Responsibility, Relationships, and Respect in Your Classroom*. ASCD. Alexandria, VA.

Danielson, Charlotte. 2007. *Enhancing Professional Practice: A Framework for Teaching*, 2nd Edition. ASCD. Alexandria, VA.

Darling-Hammond, Lisa. 2013. *Getting Teacher Evaluation Right: What Really Matters for Effectiveness and Improvement*. Teachers College Press. New York.

Gardner, Howard. 2011. *Frames of Mind: The Theory of Multiple Intelligences*. Basic Books (Perseus Books Group). New York.

Garrett, Tracey. 2014. *Effective Classroom Management: The Essentials*. Teachers College Press. New York.

Henry, Nelson B. 2012. *The Dynamics of Instructional Groups: Sociopsychological Aspects of Teaching and Learning*. Literary Licensing, LLC. Whitefish, MT.

Management Styles: Overview and Examples. Indeed Career Guide. 2020, February 14. Retrieved June 23, 2020, from indeed.com/career-advice/career-development/management-styles.

Marzano, Robert and John S. Kendall. 2007. *The New Taxonomy of Educational Objectives*, 2nd Edition. Sage Publications. Thousand Oaks, CA.

McGuire, Saundra Yancy and Stephanie McGuire. 2015. *Teach Students How to Learn: Strategies You Can Incorporate into Any Course to Improve Metacognition, Study Skills, and Motivation*. Stylus Publishing, LLC. Sterling, VA.

National Center for Education Statistics (NCES). Digest of Education Statistics. Table 204.90. Percentage of Public School Students Enrolled in Gifted and Talented Programs. Retrieved June 22, 2020, from nces.ed.gov/programs/digest/d17/tables/dt17_204.90.

Glossary of Terms

A day/B day—scheduling of students in classes on alternating days of the week

Accommodations—methods used by educators to help level the playing field for students with learning difficulties

Accountability—schools being held responsible for preparing their students to meet state and national achievement standards

Agenda—a list of the day's lesson activities in the order in which they should be completed

ALICE® (Alert, Lockdown, Inform, Counter, Evacuate)—acronym of a security training organization that provides emergency preparedness training for schools and other organizations

American College Test (ACT)—standardized college entrance examination

Anticipation guide—a graphic organizer used at the start of a lesson designed to raise student interest and expectation in the upcoming lesson

Assessment—a test, exam, standardized test, or other measurement device to determine what students have learned

Bell schedule—the scheduled times when bells signal the start or end of classes in schools

Bell-to-bell instruction—the instructional strategy of utilizing every minute of class time for learning/instruction from the starting class bell to the ending class bell

Benchmark—a standard or criteria of measurement

Blended learning—students learn by a combination of traditional instruction and online learning

Brain break—short breather in lesson activities to promote improved focus

Bullying—verbal or physical aggression intending to invoke fear or harm on someone perceived as weaker

Certification—license awarded by states to those who have completed the college degree requirements of teacher preparation programs

Charter school—school chartered by the state to provide the public with more choices of schools providing a free public education

Chromebook®—small laptop computer (powered by Google®) distributed to students for online learning

Chunking—teaching strategy that presents information to students in smaller units or chunks rather than presenting the entire idea or concept all at once

Common Core—the basic (or core) concepts and evaluation standards for the major subjects that are common to public school students in grades K–12

Confidentiality—protection of the privacy rights of students

Cooperative learning—a group of learning strategies designed to involve and engage students actively in the learning process

Cumulative—comprised of accumulated parts

Curriculum map—the sequence of the skills and content taught in a course so teachers can track what has been taught and plan what will be taught

Cyberbullying—verbal threats, slander, name-calling, posting of embarrassing photos, and other bullying behavior using electronic methods such as texting, social media, the Internet, etc.

Department—organizing the courses and teachers of the same subjects together

Department head—the faculty member assigned to lead the teachers of the same subjects/courses

Detention—consequence applied to student misbehavior usually requiring the student to stay after school is dismissed

Differentiation—an approach to teaching in which educators plan activities that account for students' different learning styles, strengths, and weaknesses

Digital textbook—a book used as the textbook for a class that is accessible on electronic devices such as tablets, laptops, or smartphones

Directed Reading Thinking Activity (DRTA)—a learning strategy used to improve reading comprehension that requires students to make predictions before they read

Disruption—an occurrence in the learning environment that interrupts students' ability to stay focused on the lesson activities

Do-now—a learning activity at the beginning of a lesson used to connect students' prior knowledge to ideas in the upcoming lesson

Edgenuity®—educational software company providing courses for online learning

Elective—classes that students may elect to take to complete a selected course of study

Elmo®—device used to magnify and project images of handouts, pages, etc. onto a large screen for student viewing

Emergency folder—folder kept in classrooms that includes information on school emergency procedures

English Language Learners (ELLs)—students whose native language is not English

Essential question (EQ)—deep, fundamental question based on the lesson content that is used to guide students' learning so they can correctly answer the essential question at the end of the learning unit

Evacuation—emergency procedure followed in case of fire, bomb threat, gas leaks, etc.

Every Student Succeeds Act (ESSA)—national law that governs K–12 public education

Exit ticket—a learning activity in which students are required to submit an answer as their ticket out the door at the end of a class

Field day—a day when regular classes are abbreviated or suspended to conduct outside recreational games and activities for students

Fire drill—fire emergency practice procedure conducted monthly

Flipped classroom—students learn lesson content by watching teaching videos at home and do the reinforcement activities in class at school

Formative—checks for understanding while the content learning is in process (being formed)

Graphic organizer—educational tool that uses a diagram or other visual display to help students organize thoughts and ideas

Hall pass—written or electronic authorization for a student to leave a classroom while classes are in session

Head of school—person who is in charge of a private school

Heterogenous grouping—grouping students together who learn at different rates

Homogenous grouping—grouping students together who learn at a similar pace

Hybrid learning—a learning model that combines in-person instruction with remote, online instruction

Inclusion—special education term indicating that students with disabilities are to be included and have equal access to a free and appropriate public education

Individualized education plan (IEP)—a written plan for a student with disabilities that clearly defines how a school plans to meet the student's special education needs

Individuals With Disabilities Education Act (IDEA)—national law protecting the education rights of students with disabilities

Infraction—misbehavior that is a violation of the school's code of conduct

Interim grade—the student's grade at the midpoint of the marking period

Interim teacher—alternate term for substitute teacher

KWL chart—What I **Know**, What I **Want** to know, What I have **Learned**—graphic organizer on which the student records what they already know and what they want to know before the learning activity and what they learned after the learning activity

Lead teacher—the faculty member assigned to lead the teachers of the same subjects/courses

Lesson plan—written plan of the lesson that includes the lesson objectives, activities, resources, and assessment

Lockdown—emergency preparedness procedure requiring occupants of the building to remain inside with doors and windows locked, windows covered, and maintaining silence

Low-stakes testing—testing that has a low impact on students' grades

Manipulatives—small objects such as blocks, chips, buttons, beads, shapes, etc. that can be easily manipulated to teach concepts and reinforce learning

Marking periods—division of the school year into separate grade reporting periods lasting from six to eight weeks each

Metacognition—analyzing how one thinks, learns, and processes information

On task—focused and working on the lesson activity

Paraprofessional—instructional aide responsible for facilitating student learning in the classroom, or noninstructional aide responsible for assisting students in hallways, cafeterias, buses, etc.

Pedagogy—the study of the science of teaching

Pep rally—assembly of students and staff to encourage the school's sports teams

Per diem—by the day; service or use by the day

Pod—a section of the school building where a certain grade level is located (i.e., sixth-grade pod)

PowerSchool®—educational administration software for recording student data electronically

Pre-K—refers to pre-kindergarten students typically between ages 2 to 5

Preliminary Scholastic Achievement Test (PSAT)—standardized college entrance examination usually administered to students in grades 10–11

Presentation software—computer software for creating presentation slides

Primary—elementary grades; kindergarten through grade 5

Private school—school funded by tuition and governed by individuals or private board of directors

Professional development (PD)—training sessions for instructional staff which may be a requirement to retain or renew teaching certificates/ licenses

Professional learning community (PLC)—team of teachers of the same subject or grade who meet periodically to exchange ideas

Public-address (PA) system—system used to broadcast announcements to every room in a building simultaneously

Public school—school that is free to the public and governed by the state

Redirect—assisting students to regain focus who have lost focus on the lesson activity

Reflective practice—practice by teachers of evaluating themselves and reflecting on teaching strategies that were effective or where improvements/changes are needed

Resource officer—police officer assigned to work in a school

Rubric—a scoring guide that defines grading standards for students' performance

Scaffolding—a teaching strategy in which students are provided with supports for learning which are then gradually removed as students demonstrate comprehension

Scholastic Achievement Test (SAT)—standardized college entrance examination usually administered to students in grades 11–12

Schoology®—educational software that teachers use to convey lessons, assignments, announcements, etc. to students electronically

Science, Technology, Engineering, and Mathematics (STEM)—an integrated area of study that includes computer science and is designed to prepare students for a variety of STEM careers

Seat chart—diagram of a classroom's seating arrangement for the students in the class

Shelter in place—emergency preparedness procedure requiring building occupants to remain in their current location with doors/windows locked or to move to a location away from windows

Smartboard—interactive teaching and electronic projection device

Social media—various platforms through which people socialize electronically

Special education—the practice of tailoring education to meet the needs of students with disabilities

Sponge—short learning activity at the end of a class session designed to use/soak up the final minutes of class time

Spreadsheet software—computer software with formula, function, and graph features for preparing numerical documents/reports

Standardized test—test administered to large numbers of students that applies the same achievement standards to all the students in a school, district, city, county, state, or country

Student growth objective (SGO)—learning goal/objective set at the start of a course for the amount of growth (learning progress) a student should show by the end of the course

Substitute teacher—person hired to stand in or substitute for a classroom teacher in his/her absence

Summative—grading/testing administered at the completion of a learning unit or course

Superintendent—person who heads a public school district

Suspension—consequence of discipline infractions requiring the student to remain out of classes or out of school for a designated period of time

Texting—cell phone communication method involving sending words/text

Virtual learning—the use of various electronic devices and software to present instruction to students/learners

Warmup—brief activity at the start of class related to the day's lesson that is designed to get students working immediately

Wi-Fi (wireless fidelity)—ability to access the Internet through radio waves rather than wires

Word processing software—computer software for creating letters, reports, and word-based documents

Word wall—display of the vocabulary of a learning unit in a way that is visually prominent and easy for all students in the classroom to see (such as on a wall or bulletin board)

Worksheet—activity on paper so students can work on learning a lesson concept/idea

Printed in the United States
By Bookmasters